Book Two

The Magic of Music

LORRAIN E. WATTERS / LOUIS G. WERSEN / WILLIAM C. HARTSHORN

L. EILEEN McMILLAN / ALICE GALLUP / FREDERICK BECKMAN

Illustrations by Aliki, Robert DeCoste, and Walt Disney Productions

GINN AND COMPANY
A XEROX COMPANY

Acknowledgments

Grateful acknowledgment is made to the following authors and publishers for permission to use and adapt copyrighted materials:

THE CURTIS PUBLISHING COMPANY and E. KATHRYN FOWLER, for "Secrets," reprinted by special permission from *Jack and Jill* Magazine © 1939 The Curtis Publishing Company.

DOUBLEDAY & COMPANY, INC., for "Singing Time," from *The Fairy Green* by Rose Fyleman. Copyright 1923 by George H. Doran Company. Reprinted by permission of Doubleday & Company, Inc. and The Society of Authors as the literary representative of the Estate of the late Rose Fyleman.

E. P. DUTTON & CO., INC., for "Good Night" (excerpt), from *The Susanna Winkle Book* by Dorothy Mason Pierce. Copyright, 1935, by E. P. Dutton & Co., Inc. Renewal, ©, 1963 by Dorothy Mason Pierce. Reprinted by permission of the publishers; and for "The House of the Mouse" (words), from *Another Here and Now Story Book* edited by Lucy Sprague Mitchell. Copyright, 1937, by E. P. Dutton & Co., Inc. Set to music and reprinted by permission of the publishers.

GINN AND COMPANY, for "The Wind" ("Have You Heard the Wind?"), from *Songs of Childhood*, copyright 1923, and for "Bells" ("Morning Bells"), from *Introductory Music*, copyright 1923, of the MUSIC EDUCATION SERIES. For "Jingle at the Windows" and "Lights," from *Tuning Up*, copyright 1936, 1943, and for "Christmastime" and "Thanksgiving Day" (words), from *Listen and Sing*, copyright 1936, 1943, of THE WORLD OF MUSIC series. For "The Bus," "The Happy River," "Here We Go Skating," and "The Wake-Up Clock," from *Singing on Our Way*, copyright 1949, 1957, 1959, and for "Out among the Fir Trees," from *Singing and Rhyming*, copyright 1950, 1957, 1959, of OUR SINGING WORLD series. For "I Like to Sing" and "Little Old Tugboat," from *We Sing and Play*, copyright 1957, of WE SING AND PRAISE series. And for "Dance-A-Story about The Magic Mountain," © 1964.

HARCOURT, BRACE & WORLD, INC., for "Balloons . . . Balloons" ("Balloons") (words), from *Whispers: And Other Poems*, © 1958, by Myra Cohn Livingston; and for "This Happy Day," from *The Little Hill*, copyright, 1949, by Harry Behn. Both reprinted by permission of Harcourt, Brace & World, Inc.

HEARST CORPORATION, for "Candle Star," by Lourena Renton Brown, reprinted by permission from the November, 1959 issue of *Good Housekeeping Magazine*. © 1959 by the Hearst Corporation.

HOUGHTON MIFFLIN COMPANY, for "The Allee Allee O," from *Hullabaloo and Other Singing Games* by Richard Chase, copyright 1949 by Houghton Mifflin Company.

HUMPTY DUMPTY, INC., for "Maytime Magic" ("Spring Magic") (words), by Mabel Watts, from *Humpty Dumpty's Magazine*, copyright 1954.

J. B. LIPPINCOTT COMPANY, for "Long Ago—Maybe a Week or So," from *All Through the Year* by Annette Wynne. Copyright 1932, 1960 by Annette Wynne; and for "Wouldn't You?" from *You Read to Me, I'll Read to You* by John Ciardi. Copyright © 1962 by John Ciardi. Both published by J. B. Lippincott Company.

ABR. LUNDQUIST AB, for "The Elves' Christmas Eve" (melody), by Wilhelm Sefve, from *Koska Meillä on Joulu*.

THE MACMILLAN COMPANY, for "A Swing Song" (excerpt), reprinted with permission of The Macmillan Company from *Robin Redbreast* by William Allingham. Copyright 1930 by The Macmillan Company.

DAVID MCKAY COMPANY, INC., for "My Mother" (words), reprinted by permission of David McKay Company, Inc., New York, from *Christopher, O!*, copyright 1947 by Barbara Young.

MEREDITH PUBLISHING COMPANY, for "Clouds" (words), by Marguerite Gode, from *Better Homes and Gardens*.

NORDISKA MUSIKFÖRLAGET, for "Nu Är Det Jul" ("Now It Is Yule"), by Irma Attermark, from *Nu Ska Vi Sjunga*, published by Hugo Gebers Förlag.

G. P. PUTNAM'S SONS, for "Evening Walk" ("Stars") (words), from *All Together* by Dorothy Aldis. Copyright 1925, 1926, 1927, 1928, 1934, 1939, 1952 by Dorothy Aldis. Reprinted by permission of G. P. Putnam's Sons.

FREDERICK WARNE & CO., INC., for "Little Wind" (words), from *Under the Window* by Kate Greenaway, used by permission of the publisher, Frederick Warne and Company.

WILLIS MUSIC COMPANY, for "Indian Lullaby," by Walter H. Aiken, used by permission of copyright owners, Willis Music Company, Cincinnati, Ohio.

WONDERLAND MUSIC CO. INC., for "If You Can't Say Something Nice," by Richard M. Sherman and Robert B. Sherman © 1963 Wonderland Music Co. Inc.; "I'll Call Him Bambi," by Richard M. Sherman and Robert B. Sherman © 1963 Wonderland Music Co. Inc.; "It's So Nice on the Ice," by Richard M. Sherman and Robert B. Sherman © 1963 Wonderland Music Co. Inc.; "Little April Shower," by Larry Morey and Frank Churchill © 1942 Wonderland Music Co. Inc.; "Spring Song," by Larry Morey and Frank Churchill © 1942 Wonderland Music Co. Inc. This arrangement © 1964 Wonderland Music Co. Inc.; and "Through the Forest," based on a theme by Frank Churchill. Adaptation, additional music, and lyrics by Richard M. Sherman and Robert B. Sherman © 1963 Wonderland Music Co. Inc.

All illustrations on pages 65, 66, 67, 68, 69, 70, 71, 72, 73, 74, 76, 77, 78, 79, 80, and 81 © Walt Disney Productions.

In the case of some material for which acknowledgment is not given, we have earnestly endeavored to find the original source and to procure permission for its use, but without success.

Contents

I LIKE MUSIC

I Like to Sing 7
March of the Little Flags 9
My Little Red Drum 10
Dance in a Circle 15
Ring-ting-tingle 17

MUSIC WE CAN SING AND PLAY

Moonlight 20
The Happy River 21
See the Little Ducklings 22
The Escalator 24
Morning Bells 25
Twinkle, Twinkle, Little Star 26
Out among the Fir Trees 28
Here We Go Skating 29
Autumn 30
One, Two, Three 31
A Rockabye Song 32
Kind Mister Cobbler 33
Moonlight 34
Go to Sleep 36
Slumber Bells 37
After School 38
Little Wind 39
The Hunter 40

MUSIC BRINGS US WONDERMENT

The Magic of Musical Sound (Unit) . . 44
Autumn Rainbow 46
Leaf Kites 47
Have You Heard the Wind? 48
Clouds 49
Little Sir Echo 50
Lights 52
Stars 53

Snowflakes 54
The Wind 56
An April Day 57
Spring Magic 58
Balloons 60
The Nightingale 62
Bye'm Bye 63
Little Man in the Wood 64

Walt Disney's BAMBI (Song Story)

Spring Song 66
I'll Call Him Bambi 69
If You Can't Say Something Nice . . . 70
Through the Forest 72
Little April Shower 75
It's So Nice on the Ice 78
Spring Song 82

MUSIC HELPS US CELEBRATE

Stand Up! 84
Happy Birthday to You 85
Hurray for Halloween! 86
Pick a Pumpkin 87
Pumpkin Face 88
Thanksgiving 89
Thanksgiving Day 90
Thank You 91
Candles Burning 92
Hanukkah Time 93
O Christmas Tree (*German*) 94
Now It Is Yule (*Swedish*) 96
Merry Christmas! (*Spanish*) 97
Christmas Cradle Song (*French*) . . . 97
The Elves' Christmas Eve 98
Christmastime 100
O Come, Little Children 101
O Come, All Ye Faithful 102

Away in a Manger 102
O Little Town of Bethlehem . . . 103
Silent Night 103
We Wish You a Merry Christmas . . 104
A Jolly Party 106
A Special Valentine 107
Beautiful Bells at Easter Time . . . 108
At Easter Time 109
I Like to Make Up Songs (Unit) . . . 110
   Bell Horses 110
   Bell Horses 111
   Early to Bed 112

The Puppet Show 138
I Know Amelia 139
Dance, Indian Man 140
Riddle Song 141
It's Music Time Again 142
Fun with Instruments (Unit) 143
   Westminster Chimes 143
   Norfolk Chimes 143
   Musette 144
   Très Jolie Waltz 144
   Debka Hora 145
   Magic Bell Song 145

MUSIC OF HOME AND COUNTRY

America, the Beautiful 114
America 115
The Star-Spangled Banner 116
Yankee Doodle 118
Our Flag 119
Daddy's Lullaby 120
Sleep, Baby, Sleep! (German) . . . 121
Dearest Child (Spanish) 122
My Mother 123
The Slumber Boat 124
Indian Lullaby 125
Little Bird on My Window 126
My Wish 127
The Wake-Up Clock 128
Tommy 129
My Donkey 130
Little Chick 131
Hideaway Bunny 132

MUSIC FROM TIP TO TOE

How Do You Do Today? 148
Dance, My Top! 150
Skip to My Lou 152
The Bus 153
Jingle at the Windows 154
Bake a Cherry Pie 156
On the Bridge of Avignon (French) . 157
To Paree (French) 158
Seesaw 159
The Allee Allee O 160
Little Old Tugboat 161
Chiapanecas 162
Rain-Dance Song 163
Big Drum and Little Drum 164
The Drum Major 166

DANCE–A–STORY

The Magic Mountain 167

Classified Index 215

My Music Dictionary 220

Alphabetical Index 222

Index of First Lines of Poems . . . 224

MUSIC FOR FUN

The Hen Who Quacked 134
Six Little Ducks 135
The House of the Mouse 136
Music Time (Unit) 137
   It's Music Time Again 137

I Like Music

I like to sing . . .

I Like to Sing

Sheila Galvin

Mexican Folk Melody

I like to sing when the sun is shin - ing,

I like to sing tra la la la lee;_____

I like to sing when the rain is fall - ing,

I like to sing tra la la la lee. _____

This is a song.

A song has words and music.

I like to march . . .

March of the Little Flags

Adapted by H. G. W.

Olga B. Pohlmann

In marching tempo

March - ing, march - ing, flags are march - ing,

Col - ors fly - ing bright and gay. ____

Like lit - tle sol - diers we're march - ing at play;

Soon lit - tle flags will be march - ing a - way.

This is the way to march:

left, right, left, right.

I like to play the drum . . .

My Little Red Drum

Ena B. Knippel

I march down the street with my new red drum,

Tum - tum - tum - tum - tum!

I smile and I wave at the friends I meet,

Tum - tum - tum - tum - tum!

Here we come! Here we come!

Tum - tum - tum - tum - tum!

Here we come! Here we come!

Tum - tum - tum - tum - tum!

I like to listen . . .

There's magic in music,
There's magic in sound;
There's magic in beauty
Wherever it's found.

L. E. Watters

Dance in a Circle

Katherine S. Bolt

Italian Folk Melody

Dance in a cir - cle and sing a-long to -geth - er.

Dance in a cir - cle and sing a-long to - day.

To the cen-ter, *stamp your feet!* *

Back a-gain and *stamp your feet!*

Turn in your plac - es and bow a-cross the way.

*Other actions such as *clap your hands* or *shake your head* may be used.

I like to play the bells . . .

Ring-ting-tingle

H. F. G.

American Folk Melody

Rhythmically

I   can   play,   ring - ting - tin - gle,

You   can   play,   ring - ting - tin - gle,

We   can   play,   ring - ting - tin - gle,

Let's   all   play   the   bells.

I want to learn all about music . . .

I want to make up poems and songs.

I want to learn to read music.

Music We Can Sing and Play

This song has only three different *tones*.
The *home tone* is C.

Moonlight

Helen Taylor

French Folk Melody

Quietly

When the day is o - ver

Comes a sil - ver light.

High the moon is shin - ing

Through the qui - et night.

How many different tones are in this song?

The Happy River

L. B. P.

French Folk Melody

Not too slowly

Hear   the   hap - py   riv - er

Sing - ing,   sing - ing,

Hear   the   hap - py   riv - er

Sing - ing   as   it   flows.

21

There are six different tones in this song.
Which is the home tone?

See the Little Ducklings

German Folk Song

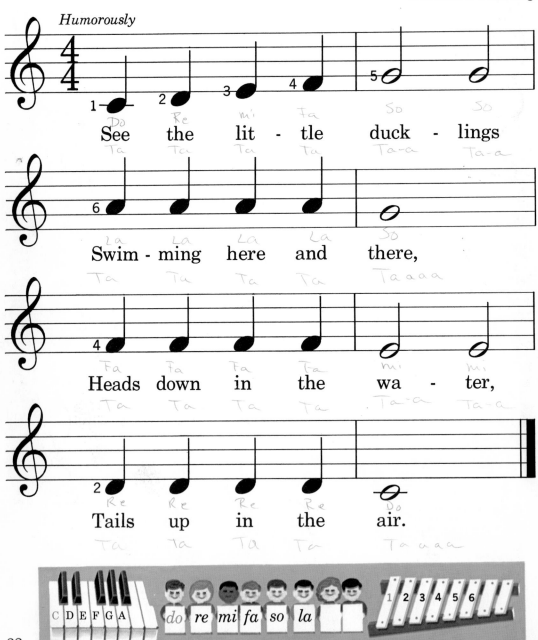

How many different tones are there in this song?

The Escalator

Scale Song

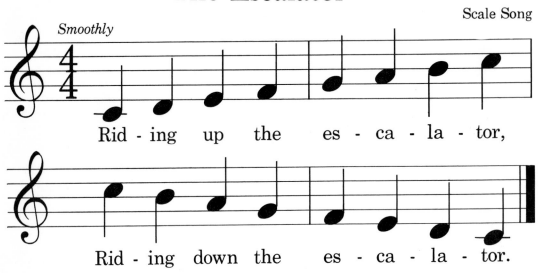

Smoothly

Rid - ing up the es - ca - la - tor,

Rid - ing down the es - ca - la - tor.

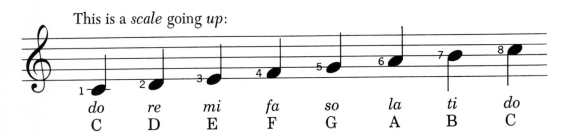

This is a *scale* going *up*:

1	2	3	4	5	6	7	8
do	*re*	*mi*	*fa*	*so*	*la*	*ti*	*do*
C	D	E	F	G	A	B	C

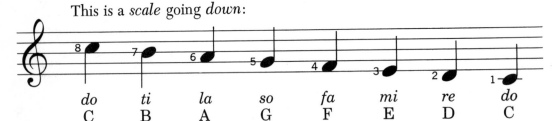

This is a *scale* going *down*:

8	7	6	5	4	3	2	1
do	*ti*	*la*	*so*	*fa*	*mi*	*re*	*do*
C	B	A	G	F	E	D	C

C D E F G A B C   *do re mi fa so la ti do*   1 2 3 4 5 6 7 8

Where do you find a scale in this song?
Does it go up or down?

Morning Bells

Lena Chase

Folk Melody

Cheerfully

Morn - ing   bells   are   gai - ly   ring - ing,

Ding,   dong,   ding,   dong;

High   up   in   the   bel - fry   swing - ing,

Ding,   ding,   dong.

Twinkle, Twinkle, Little Star

Traditional

Twin - kle, twin - kle, lit - tle star,

How I won - der what you are!

Up a - bove the world so high,

Like a dia - mond in the sky.

Twin - kle, twin - kle, lit - tle star,

How I won - der what you are!

When you read this poem or sing this song, some *words* and some *notes* are held longer than others. Clap or tap as you sing. The *steady* notes you are tapping are called *quarter notes.*

quarter note   half note

You find that the *longer* notes need two taps. These notes are called *half notes.* Half notes get two taps or *beats* as you sing the words below them.

Out among the Fir Trees

Translated

Czech Folk Song

Not too slowly

Out a - mong the fir trees,

Ev - er - green and pine trees,

Wool - ly sheep are graz - ing While the

shep - herds watch at ease.

Find the notes that get one beat, two beats. The last note is a *whole note*. It gets four beats.

whole note

Here We Go Skating

L. B. P.

French Folk Melody

Here we go skat-ing a - long in a row,

Skat-ing and skat-ing and skat-ing we go.

Are you skating up or down the hill? Can you find a "hump" along the way? As you sing, show with your hand the direction of the *melody*.

The *dotted half note* gets three beats in this song.

dotted half note

29

Autumn

L. E. W.

Ludwig van Beethoven

Lightly

Leaves of red, o - ver - head,

Tell us au-tumn is com - ing.

Leaves of brown, tum - bling down,

Tell us au-tumn is here. _____

With your hand show how the melody goes up and down.
Which notes are *higher*? Which notes are *lower*?

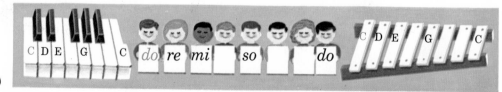

One, Two, Three

Carol Davis

One, two, three, Mon - key in a tree,

Two, three, four, Hear the li - ons roar,

Three, four, five, Hon - ey in a hive,

Six, sev'n, eight, Hur - ry don't be late!

As you sing the song, clap or tap the beat. Notice that sometimes there are two notes for one beat. They are called *eighth notes.*

eighth notes

The home tone is C (*do*).

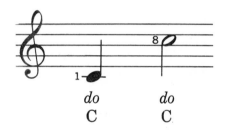

do C *do* C

31

Should this lullaby be sung *loudly* or *softly*? Why?

A Rockabye Song

Katherine S. Bolt

Uruguayan Folk Melody

Gently

Go to sleep, my ba - by,

Close your drow - sy eyes.

I will rock you gen - tly,

Sing - ing lul - la - bies.

What kinds of notes are these?

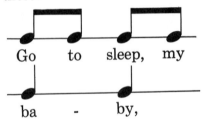

Go to sleep, my ba - by,

32

Kind Mister Cobbler

Freely Translated

Argentine Folk Song

Smoothly

Kind Mis-ter Cob-bler, Can you fix my shoe?

Kind Mis-ter Cob-bler, Make it good as new.

The home tone is C. On what tone does the song begin? On what tone does it end? Notice that the second line of the melody looks almost like the first. How is it different?

Tap these *rhythms:*

Do you remember this song on page 20 when the home tone
was C and you sang it with your low voice? This is the same
song, but now the home tone is F. The notes *look higher* and
the song *sounds higher*.

Moonlight

Helen Taylor

French Folk Melody

When the day is o - ver

Comes a sil - ver light.

High the moon is shin - ing

Through the qui - et night.

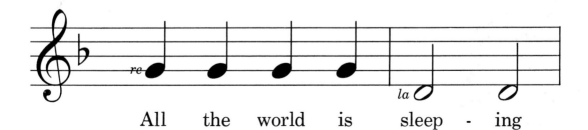

re ♩ ♩ ♩ ♩   *la* ○   ○

All   the   world   is   sleep - ing

re ♩ *do* ♩ *ti* ♩ *la* ♩ *so* ○

In   the   sil - ver   light.

High   the   moon   is   shin - ing

Through   the   qui - et   night.

C D E F G A   *so la ti do re mi*   C D E F G A

This song has only four different tones.
What is the name of the home tone?

Go to Sleep

Spanish Folk Song

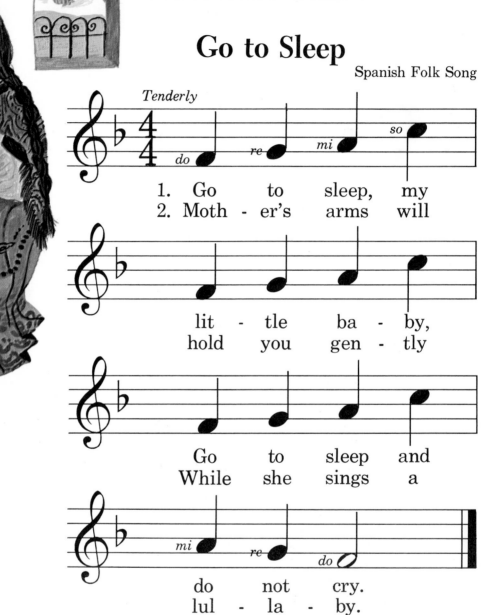

Tenderly

do re mi so

1. Go   to   sleep,   my
2. Moth - er's   arms   will

lit - tle   ba - by,
hold   you   gen - tly

Go   to   sleep   and
While   she   sings   a

mi re do

do   not   cry.
lul - la - by.

F G A C   do re mi   so   F G A C

36

How many different tones are in this song?

Slumber Bells

Translated

Basque Melody

Slowly

mi Ding,   dong,   ding, dong, ding,

Lit - tle bells will be - gin to ring.

Ding,   dong,   ding, dong, ding,

Chil - dren soon will be slum - ber - ing.

Watch the notes while you sing and gently clap or tap the beat. Find the places where there are

two beats to one note (♩) ,

one beat to one note (♩) , and

two notes for one beat (♫) .

After School

Grace Boynton

Chinese Folk Melody

School is___ out as the sun goes down;

Books in my bag I go through the town.

Home are my par - ents who smile at me;

I make a nice low bow like this, you see.

Each line of this song is a *musical phrase*. A musical phrase gives a musical idea or thought. How many phrases are there in this song? What kind of note do you find at the end of each phrase?

As you sing, tap the rhythm of the melody using sticks or wood blocks.

Little Wind

Kate Greenaway

Ruth Stapp

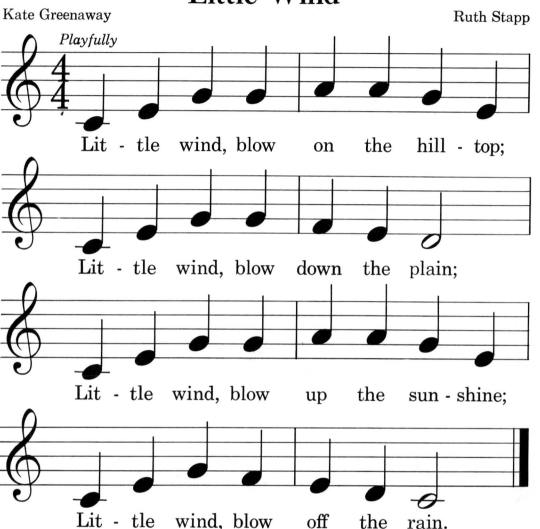

Playfully

Lit - tle wind, blow on the hill - top;

Lit - tle wind, blow down the plain;

Lit - tle wind, blow up the sun - shine;

Lit - tle wind, blow off the rain.

When the first three tones of this melody are played at the same time, they form a *chord*.

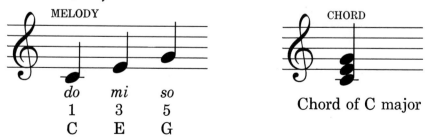

MELODY

do mi so
1   3   5
C   E   G

CHORD

Chord of C major

The Hunter

Marian Major

French Folk Song

Brightly

1,2. Care - ful, all you fur - ry friends,

Dan - ger for you nev - er ends.

1. There's a hun - ter in the wood.
2. Soon the hun - ter, oh so sly,

He would catch you if he could,
Sure - ly will be pass - ing by.

So do be care - ful, lit - tle friends.

Re - mem - ber, dan - ger nev - er ends.

When the first four tones of this melody are played at the same time, they form a chord. Since the chord is built on C, it is called a C chord.

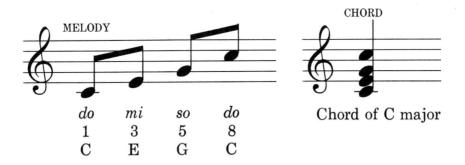

MELODY

do   mi   so   do
1   3   5   8
C   E   G   C

CHORD

Chord of C major

These measures are taken from songs you have learned. Can you name the songs?

Music Brings Us Wonderment

The Magic of Musical Sound

The sound of music is one of the most beautiful sounds you will ever hear. You can not see it or touch it. You can only hear it. At times it seems to be coming from far, far away. Musical tones sometimes have a magical power. When you really listen to them, you may feel you are taking a trip on a magic carpet to a world of wonderful sound. Listen to the beautiful tones of the stringed instruments as they play the "Pastoral Symphony" from Handel's *Messiah*.

The Violin and Bow
A Stringed Instrument

The violin is the smallest and best known member of the *stringed instrument family*. When a bow is drawn over them, the four strings of the violin can make lovely tones.

There are many kinds of musical sound. Some of them come from stringed instruments. Some of them come from instruments called wind instruments, which the player must blow. There are two groups of wind instruments: the *woodwind family* and the *brass family*. Their playing can be very exciting. Listen to the bright sound of the wind instruments in Kodaly's tonal picture of the "Viennese Musical Clock."

The Flute
A Woodwind Instrument

The Trumpet
A Brass Instrument

Another family of instruments is the *percussion family*. Drums and other instruments which are struck belong to this family. Which percussion instruments can you hear in the "Viennese Musical Clock"?

The Cymbals
Percussion Instrument

The Triangle
Percussion Instrument

Autumn Rainbow

Ena B. Knippel

Freely

Au - tumn leaves up - on the ground,

Like a rain - bow up - side down.

Their col - ors glow a - long the street,

A love - ly car - pet for my feet. ___

How does this melody suggest the shape of a rainbow? As you sing each phrase, draw a beautiful rainbow in the air.

Leaf Kites

Marguerite Gode

R. Ena Butler

Gracefully

Fair - ies are fly - ing their leaf kites to - day,

Out in the woods where the wind is at play.

Red ones and yel - low, Or - ange and brown,

Way up in the air they go sail - ing, then down.

What are leaf kites? Do they sail up and down? Where does the melody move up and down?

If I
Could go
As high
And low
As the wind
As the wind
As the wind
Can blow—

I'd go!

John Ciardi

Have You Heard the Wind?

Will Earhart

Have you heard the wind go "Oo," _____

Blow-ing down the chim - ney, "Oo," _____

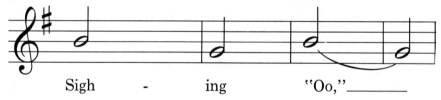

Sigh - ing "Oo," _____

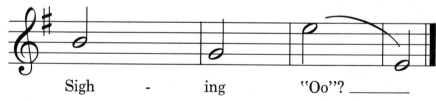

Sigh - ing "Oo"? _____

Sometimes the wind's song moves up
eight tones. This is called an *octave.*

Play these tones softly on resonator
bells. Where in the song does the wind
move up an octave? Down an octave?

As you play the bells, make your voice
sound like the wind. Can you "make up"
a song about the wind?

OCTAVE

E   E

48

Clouds

Marguerite Gode

George K. Seiler

Gently

Some-where a   jol - ly   old   gi - ant must   be

Blow-ing soap   bub-bles for   chil-dren to   see,

Blow-ing soap   bub-bles and toss-ing them high,—

To make them go   sail-ing a - cross the blue sky.

49

Little Sir Echo

Original Version by
Laura R. Smith and
J. S. Fearis

Revised Arrangement by
Adele Girard and
Joe Marsala

Lightly

1. Lit - tle Sir Ech - o, how do you do,
2. Lit - tle Sir Ech - o, you're ver - y near,

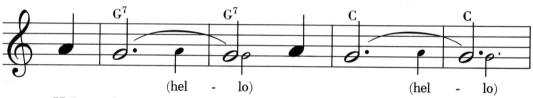

(hel - lo)   (hel - lo)

Hel - lo, _____ hel - lo, _____

Lit - tle Sir Ech - o, how do you do,
Lit - tle Sir Ech - o, you're ver - y clear,

(hel - lo)   (hel - lo)

Hel - lo, _____ hel - lo. _____

50

Who is Little Sir Echo?
Is his song louder or softer than yours?

A candle looked up at the sky and said,
"What is it like to be a star?"
A star smiled down from overhead
And said, "You are."

Lourena Renton Brown

Lights

Hope Ann Rhodes

Franz Joseph Haydn

Slowly

1. See my can - dle burn - ing With a gold - en light,
2. I can light a can - dle, God can light a star;

Shin-ing from my win - dow Out in - to the night!
Both of them are help - ful, Shin-ing where they are.

How is the second line of Haydn's
song like the first? How is it different?

A *quarter rest* tells you to be silent
for one beat in this song.

quarter rest

52

Stars

Dorothy Aldis

Mary Duncan

Slowly

The stars were shin - ing mer - ri - ly,

A sil - ver eye, each one.

And when I ran they fol - lowed me.

So then I did - n't run.

a little slower

But lat - er when I lay in bed

Finger cymbals

They winked at me in - stead.

Why is the last phrase lower and slower than the first two phrases?
What makes the melody wink?

53

Snowflakes

Ruth-Esther Hillila

I can-not reach the stars, Yet they come down to me,

When in each shin-y snow-flake A lit-tle star I see.

They spar - kle bright - ly,

They drift so light - ly.

I turn my face up

To feel them fall.

I can-not reach the stars, Yet they come down to me,

When in each shin - y snow-flake A lit - tle star I see.

Why does the melody of the first line move up, then down? Sometimes the melody is silent and you can hear each snowflake fall (finger cymbals).

These rests (𝄽 and 𝄾) tell you when the melody is silent.

The Wind

Ardith Shelley

Smoothly

"Oo," _____ went the wind one day,

We all lis-tened care-ful - ly to hear what it would say,

"Oo, _____ Oo, _____

Oo, _____ Oo."

In what way is the second phrase like the first?

What does the wind sing in this song? Can you "make up" your own wind song?

An April Day

E. B. Kay

A-pril show-ers bring May flow-ers, So they say! So they say!

Sun-ny hours, rain - y show-ers, So they say! So they say!

What a fun-ny, mixed-up, turn-a-bout, Hap-py A- pril day!

If you know these *patterns*, you should be able to read the first two lines of this song.

This pattern moves by chord.

do	mi	so	do
1	3	5	8
C	E	G	C

This pattern moves by scale.

so	fa	mi	re
5	4	3	2
G	F	E	D

How does this pattern move?

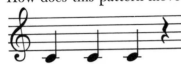

Spring Magic

Mabel Watts

Kay Stratton

Gently

A lit - tle seed for me to sow,

A lit - tle earth to make it grow,

A lit - tle hole, a lit - tle pat,

A lit - tle wish, and that is that.

A lit - tle sun, a lit - tle show - er,

A lit - tle while, and then a flow - er.

Clap or tap this rhythm pattern. How many times do you find it in this song?

This sign (⌢) tells you to *hold* the tone a little longer.

58

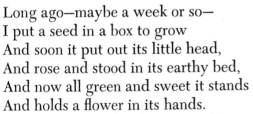

Long ago—maybe a week or so—
I put a seed in a box to grow
And soon it put out its little head,
And rose and stood in its earthy bed,
And now all green and sweet it stands
And holds a flower in its hands.
Annette Wynne

Balloons

Myra Cohn Livingston

Mary Scott King

Gracefully

Bal - loons, bal - loons on col - ored string

Are blow - ing out in - to the spring.

Bal - loons, bal - loons filled up with air

Are sail - ing off to ev - 'ry - where.

Bal - loons, bal - loons all bright and round

Are float - ing up with - out a sound. __

Where does the balloon melody sail up an octave?
Where does the balloon melody float up the scale?
Where do the balloons go at the end of the song?
As you sing, let your arms sway and gently push the floating bal-
loons.

61

The Nightingale

F. B.

French-Canadian Folk Melody

Cheerfully

By the sing - ing foun-tain hear the night - in - gale

With his love - ly mu - sic tell a fair - y tale.

"Tra la la la la la la la,

Tra la la la la la la la,"

Sings the night - in - gale.

Each time you sing this pattern in the song, play it on the bells.

mi   re   do
3   2   1
A   G   F

When part of the melody is be-tween the *repeat signs*, sing that part once again.

repeat signs

62

Bye'm Bye

American Folk Song

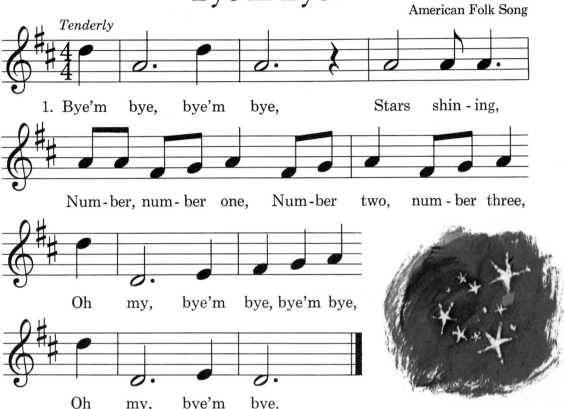

Tenderly

1. Bye'm bye, bye'm bye, Stars shin - ing,

Num - ber, num - ber one, Num - ber two, num - ber three,

Oh my, bye'm bye, bye'm bye,

Oh my, bye'm bye.

2. Bye'm bye, bye'm bye,
Stars shining,
Number, number four,
Number five, number six,
Oh my, bye'm bye, bye'm bye,
Oh my, bye'm bye.

3. Bye'm bye, bye'm bye,
Stars shining,
Number, number sev'n,
Number eight, number nine,
Oh my, bye'm bye, bye'm bye,
Oh my, bye'm bye.

Stars twinkle in the quiet night. When you count the stars as you sing, make them twinkle with finger cymbals or a triangle.

This octave may remind you of a falling star. How many "falling stars" do you see in this melody?

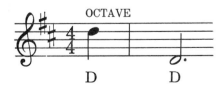

OCTAVE

D   D

63

Little Man in the Wood

From *Hansel and Gretel,*
Engelbert Humperdinck

Translated

1. There stands a lit - tle man in the deep, dark wood;
2. He stands there on one leg bend - ing to and fro;

He wears a pur - ple cloak and a small black hood.
And all that he can do is to stand and grow.

Do you know him, stand-ing there si - lent-ly, with-out a care?
Do you know him, stand-ing there in the cloak he likes to wear?

Do you see him stand-ing in the deep, dark wood?
Can you see him stand-ing in the deep, dark wood?

Who is the little man in the wood? Do you know the story of
Hansel and Gretel? When you sing, the words should be clear. Then
everyone will understand your story.

Which lines in this song are different from the first line?

Walt Disney's
BAMBI

Based on the original story by Felix Salten

This is the story of Bambi, the baby deer. Bambi was born in the forest on a beautiful morning in early spring.

Spring Song

Larry Morey   Frank Churchill

Brightly

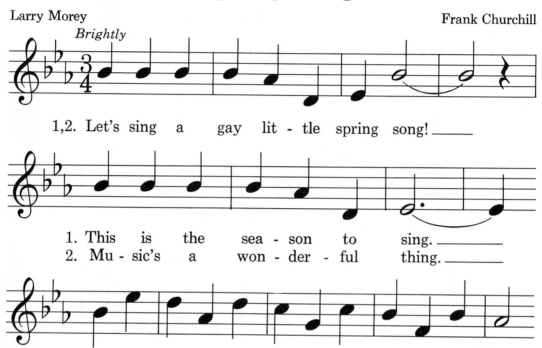

1,2. Let's sing a gay lit - tle spring song! _____

1. This is the sea - son to sing. _____
2. Mu - sic's a won - der - ful thing. _____

For things al-ways seem right when it's sun - ny and bright,
So come on and re - joice at the top of your voice,

So let's sing a song a - bout spring, spring, spring, spring,
And let's sing a song a - bout spring, spring, spring, spring,

Let's sing a song a - bout spring! ___

On that bright spring day it was Mrs. Magpie who was the first to find out about Bambi. Now Mrs. Magpie was a great chatterbox, and it didn't take her long to spread the exciting news. First she flew to Old Mr. Owl, who was just settling down for a good day's sleep.

"Old Mr. Owl," she said, "there is a new prince in the forest! A baby deer has been born."

"Whoo, whoo?" asked Old Mr. Owl, opening one eye. But Mrs. Magpie had already flown away to tell all the other forest creatures—the chipmunks and the woodchucks, the raccoons and the possums, and even the little skunk who lived behind the blackberry bush.

So Old Mr. Owl opened his other eye and flew to the little thicket where everyone was gathering. Sure enough, there was a tiny, spotted, baby deer lying by his mother's side.

"Congratulations," said Old Mr. Owl to the mother deer. "This is quite an occasion for all of us. It isn't often that a prince is born in the forest. What are you going to name him?"

And the mother said, "I think I'll call him . . . Bambi."

I'll Call Him Bambi

Richard M. Sherman
Robert B. Sherman

Tenderly

I'll call him Bam - bi, My lit - tle fawn.

He'll chase the sun - beams Spar - kling at dawn.

I'll call him Bam - bi, And when he's grown,

Brave, tall and proud he'll stand,

Prince of the for - est land,

Just like his fa - ther lit - tle Bam - bi will be.

With her nose the mother deer gently nudged her sleeping baby until he lifted his head and looked around. She nudged him again, and he pushed up on his thin legs, trying to stand.

"Look, he's trying to get up! He's awfully wobbly though, isn't he?" laughed a little rabbit named Thumper.

"Thumper!" the mother rabbit said, pulling him back. "That's not a pleasant way to talk. Remember what your father always says!"

Thumper hung his head and repeated, "If you can't say something nice, say nothing."

If You Can't Say Something Nice

Richard M. Sherman
Robert B. Sherman

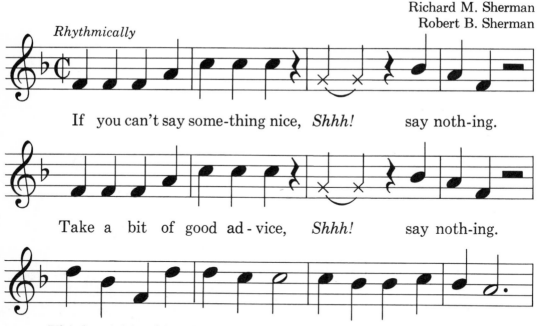

If you can't say some-thing nice, *Shhh!* say noth-ing.

Take a bit of good ad-vice, *Shhh!* say noth-ing.

Think of friend-ly things to say, That's the path to fol-low.

When you think un-friend-ly thoughts, Close your lips and swal-low!

If you think it o - ver twice, And you can't say some-thing nice,

Then don't say an - y-thing at all! *Shhh!*

The little fawn's legs were not very steady, but soon he was able to stand beside his mother. Now all the watching animals could see the white spots on his red-brown coat, and the shy look on his sleepy face. And so, having welcomed the new little prince, they began to slip quietly away. Thumper was the very last to go.

"Good-by, little Bambi," he whispered.

A baby deer has a lot to learn, and it wasn't long before
Bambi's mother was teaching him the ways of the forest.

Through the Forest

Richard M. Sherman
Robert B. Sherman

Frank Churchill

Gently

Through   the   for - est,   round   the   mead - ows,

Bam - bi would run   and   jump and   play,

While   his   moth - er   watched him   grow - ing

Strong-er   and   wis - er   ev - 'ry   day.

One day when Bambi was following his mother down a narrow forest path, they met Thumper playing with his brothers and sisters. Thumper, who always liked to show off, raced ahead and pounded his hind foot on a hollow log.

"See, Bambi, I'm thumping," he called. "That's why they call me Thumper."

Bambi pranced along behind his little friend. Suddenly he stopped to stare at a blue jay who was scolding in a loud voice.

"That's a bird," Thumper told Bambi.

"B-i-r-d," repeated Bambi, very carefully.

"He's learning to talk!" shouted Thumper.

Bambi was very proud of himself. He stopped to sniff a yellow buttercup. "Bird," he said, thinking everything was a bird.

"No, no," Thumper corrected him. "That's a flower."

Bambi sniffed some more, and just then found himself nose to nose with a little black and white skunk.

"Flower," said Bambi, and everyone burst out laughing.

"That's all right," smiled the little skunk. "He can call me Flower if he wants to." And that was how Flower got his name, even though he really didn't smell anything like a flower.

The soft sound of rain started to fill the forest. Bambi blinked his eyes. He was getting all wet.

"That's all right, Bambi," said Thumper. "It's just a little April shower."

Little April Shower

Larry Morey

Frank Churchill

Lightly

Drip, drip, drop, lit - tle A - pril show - er,

Beat - ing a tune ev - 'ry - where that you fall.

Drip, drip, drop, lit - tle A - pril show - er,

We're get - ting wet and we don't care at all.

Drip! Drop! Drip! Drop!

We're get - ting wet and we don't care at all.

The shower passed quickly, and so did all the lovely days of spring and summer. Bambi and his friend Thumper explored the meadows and the woodland pools and had such good times that they hardly knew summer was ending.

It doesn't take long for winter to come in the forest, once it makes up its mind. One morning Bambi awoke to find the ground covered with white.

"That's snow," said Thumper. "It's about time for some of our friends to take a nap."

"Nap?" asked Bambi.

"Yes," said Thumper. "In the winter most everyone in the forest goes away or takes a long nap."

And when the winter wind blew great drifts of snow, sure enough, most of Bambi's friends were nowhere to be seen—the chipmunks and the woodchucks, the raccoons and the possums, and even Flower, who lived behind the blackberry bush. But Thumper was still there. He and Bambi had a wonderful time making footprints in the snow and sliding on the ice.

It's So Nice on the Ice

Richard M. Sherman
Robert B. Sherman

With a lilt

It's so nice ____ on the ice, ____

As you glide, glide, glide. ____

It's so nice ____ on the ice, ____

As you slide, slide, slide. ____

78

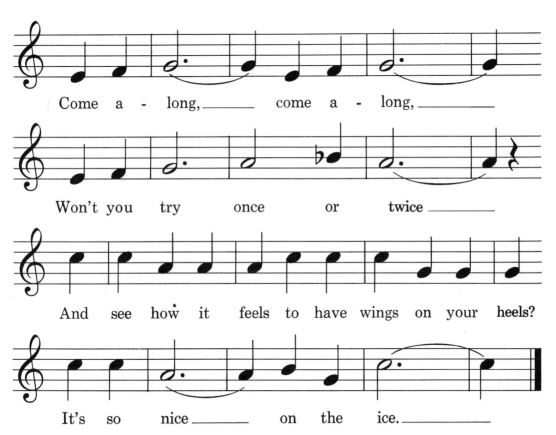

Come a - long,_____ come a - long,_____

Won't you try once or twice _____

And see how it feels to have wings on your heels?

It's so nice _____ on the ice. _____

But Bambi soon found that winter wasn't all fun. The leaves that he liked to eat had been blown away by the wind, and the mosses were covered with snow, so he was always hungry. Sometimes he thought that spring would never come. The forest seemed still and silent, and Bambi was very, very lonely.

Then one day Bambi's mother found a little patch of new grass pushing up through the snow.

"Bambi," she called. "Look! Do you know what this means? Spring is coming! Go and tell Mrs. Magpie to wake up all your friends."

So Bambi raced through the forest to find Mrs. Magpie, who spread the news in no time at all. Soon the chipmunks and the woodchucks, the raccoons and the possums, and even Flower, who lived behind the blackberry bush, were back again.

"Spring is coming!" sang the birds who had just returned from the southland.

Thumper thumped on his hollow log and shouted, "Spring is coming!"

Old Mr. Owl opened one eye and asked, "Whoo, whoo is coming?" Then all the birds and the animals answered, "Spring! Spring is coming!"

80

Bambi's friends started to laugh and dance and talk all at once. They were so happy to be together again.

But the happiest of them all was Bambi.

Spring Song

Larry Morey

Frank Churchill

Brightly

1,2. Let's sing a gay lit - tle spring song!_____

1. This is the sea - son to sing._____
2. Mu - sic's a won - der - ful thing._____

For things al-ways seem right when it's sun - ny and bright,
So come on and re - joice at the top of your voice,

So let's sing a song a - bout spring, spring, spring, spring,
And let's sing a song a - bout spring, spring, spring, spring,

Let's sing a song a - bout spring!____

THE END

Music Helps Us Celebrate

Stand Up!

Alice Ricky

Lively

Stand up if to-day is your birth-day,

Stand up if to-day is your birth-day,

Stand up if to-day is your birth-day,

Stand up! Stand up!

Happy Birthday to You

Mildred J. Hill

With spirit

Hap-py Birth-day to you, Hap-py Birth-day to you,

Hap-py Birth-day, dear _____, Hap-py Birth-day to you!

Count the age of the birthday child:

Melody and percussion instruments

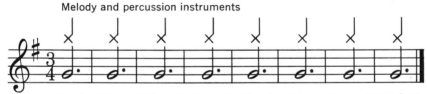

One! Two! Three! Four! Five! Six! Seven! Eight!

Owls and witches,
Spooks and cats
Have on Halloween
Masks and hats.

But I know,
I do, I do,
Behind the mask
It's really you!

E. K. Merriam

Hurray for Halloween!

Mysteriously

Elizabeth E. Rogers

Hur - ray for Hal - low - een!

Hur - ray for Hal - low - een!

Cats howl, *(meow)* and owls hoot, *(whooo)*

And witch - es fly up in the sky.

Hur - ray for Hal - low - een! *Boo!*

86

Pick a Pumpkin

Naomi Caldwell

Rhythmically

Pick a, pick a pump - kin from the pile,

We can make his eyes and a great big smile.

Pick a, pick a pump - kin round and clean,

Then we'll be read - y for Hal - low - een!

Hal-low-een, Hal-low-een, Then we'll be read-y for Hal - low-een!

Clap the beats as you say the words.

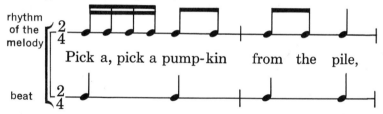

87

Pumpkin Face

Georgia Deal

Ruth Stapp

Pump-kin face, pump-kin face, look at me,

One eye's crook-ed as it can be.

Pump-kin face, pump-kin face, please hold still,

Dad-dy will fix you, I know he will.

Pump-kin face, pump-kin face, now you're done,

It's time to light the can-dle for Hal-low-een fun.

How many times is this pat-tern in the song?

Thanksgiving

Edith Krohner

Steadily

This is a time for Thanks-giv-ing, Thanks-giv-ing.

What does it mean? What does it mean?

All of our thanks to be giv - ing, be giv - ing.

This is Thanks-giv-ing to me. _____

Every morning when the sun
Comes smiling up on everyone,
It's lots of fun
To say good morning to the sun.
  Good morning, Sun!

Every evening after play
When the sunshine goes away,
It's nice to say,
Thank you for this happy day,
  This happy day!

Harry Behn

Thanksgiving Day

Mildred Adair

Olga Tock

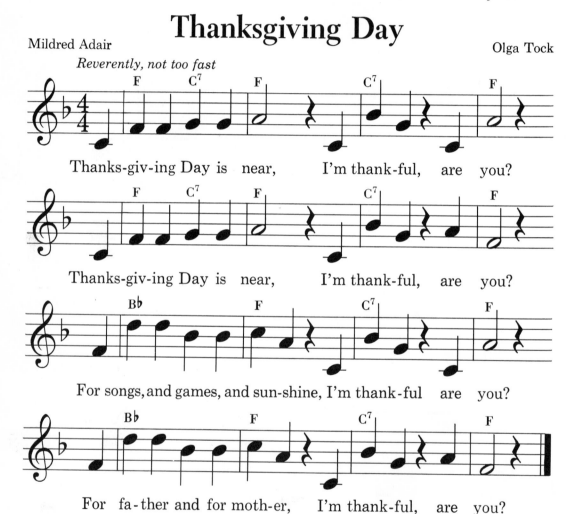

Reverently, not too fast

Thanks-giv-ing Day is near,   I'm thank-ful,   are   you?

Thanks-giv-ing Day is near,   I'm thank-ful,   are   you?

For songs, and games, and sun-shine, I'm thank-ful   are   you?

For fa-ther and for moth-er,   I'm thank-ful,   are   you?

Which lines of this song are alike?

Do you remember that a quarter rest tells you to be silent for one beat?

90

Thank You

Unknown

Franz Schubert

With devotion

Thank You for the world so sweet,

Thank You for the food we eat,

Thank You for the birds that sing,

Thank You, God, for ev - 'ry - thing.

How many times do you find this rhythm pattern in Schubert's beautiful song?

Notice that the second line of his melody is one step lower than the first line. What did Schubert do in the third line?

Candles Burning

Judith M. Berman

Not too slowly

Can - dles, can - dles burn - ing __ bright,

Tell us what is in your __ light.

Friends and dear ones are all so __ gay, __

Sing - ing the songs of hol - i - day!

Hanukkah Time

Nathan Saxon

1. Light the can - dles, Light the can - dles,

Light the can - dles at Ha - nuk - kah time.

2. Spin your dreydl,
   Spin your dreydl,
   Spin your dreydl at Hanukkah time.

3. Dance together,
   Dance together,
   Dance together at Hanukkah time.

O Christmas Tree
(O Tannenbaum)

From the German   German Carol

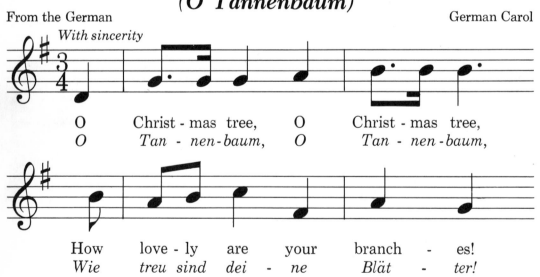

O   Christ - mas tree,   O   Christ - mas tree,
O   Tan - nen-baum,   O   Tan - nen-baum,

How   love - ly   are   your   branch - es!
Wie   treu sind dei - ne   Blät - ter!

Pronounce: *Oh tahn-en-bowm, oh tahn-en-bowm,*
Vee troy zint dy-neh bleh-tuhr!

O Christ - mas tree, O Christ - mas tree,
O Tan - nen-baum, O Tan - nen-baum,

How love - ly are your branch - es!
Wie treu sind dei - ne Blät - ter!

In sum - mer sun or win - ter snow,

A dress of green you al - ways show,

O Christ - mas tree, O Christ - mas tree,
O Tan - nen-baum, O Tan - nen-baum,

How love - ly are your branch - es!
Wie treu sind dei - ne Blät - ter!

Children in Germany still sing this carol at Christmastime. The custom of bringing a Christmas tree into the home came from Germany.

Now It Is Yule
(Nu Är Det Jul)

Irma Attermark

Happily

Now it is Yule in all the house,

Christ-mas bells are ring - ing.

Lights are shin - ing through the house.

Start the car - ol sing - ing.

Now it is Yule, now it is Yule, Now it is Yule.
Nu är det Jul, nu är det Jul, Nu är det Jul.

Pronounce: *Noo awr det yool.*

School children in Sweden enjoy this happy holiday song.

96

Merry Christmas!
(¡Feliz Navidad!)

Maria Mendoza

¡Fe - liz Na - vi - dad! ¡Fe - liz Na - vi - dad!

Mer - ry Christ - mas, ev - 'ry - one!

Pronounce: *Fay-lees nah-vee-dahd.*

Christmas Cradle Song

Eleanor M. Edwards

Dors, dors, dors, Pe - tit Fils.

Sleep, lit - tle Child, in love and peace.

Dors, dors, ___ dors, Pe - tit Fils.

Pronounce: *Dor, dor, dor, puh-tee fees.*

The Elves' Christmas Eve

Translated by
Ruth-Esther Hillila

Wilhelm Sefve

Lightly

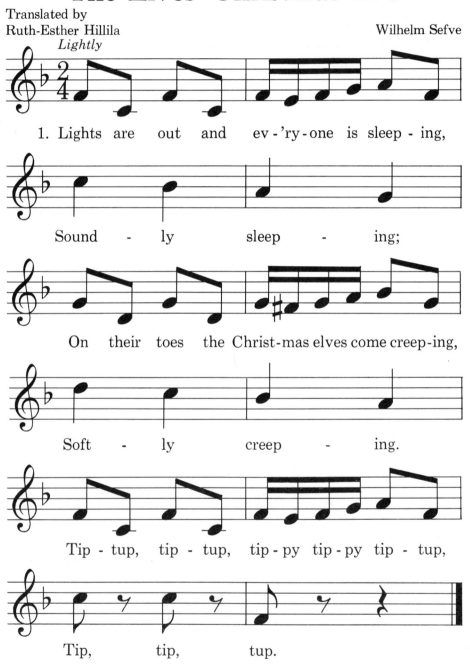

1. Lights are out and ev-'ry-one is sleep - ing,

Sound - ly sleep - ing;

On their toes the Christ-mas elves come creep-ing,

Soft - ly creep - ing.

Tip - tup, tip - tup, tip-py tip-py tip - tup,

Tip, tip, tup.

2. From the cracks and corners they come hopping, They come hopping;
   When they see the food there is no stopping, Is no stopping.
   Tip-tup, etc.

3. One by one they climb upon the table, On the table;
   Here they eat as much as they are able, They are able.
   Tip-tup, etc.

4. Round the goodies all the elves are skipping, Elves are skipping;
   In the pudding each a finger dipping, Finger dipping.
   Tip-tup, etc.

5. Now beneath the Christmas tree there's dancing, There is dancing;
   Holding hands, the little elves are prancing, Elves are prancing.
   Tip-tup, etc.

6. Leaving all the folk still soundly sleeping, Soundly sleeping;
   To their homes the Christmas elves go creeping, Elves go creeping.
   Tip-tup, etc.

If you see a package
Gaily wrapped and tied,
Don't ask too many questions,
'Cause a secret is inside.

E. Kathryn Fowler

Christmastime

Ethel Crowninshield

Brightly

1. I like the Christ-mas-time for lots of dif-f'rent things;
2. Moth - er will hang a wreath of hol - ly on our door,

I like the Christ-mas songs that ev-'ry-bod - y sings.
As she has done each year at Christ-mas-time be -fore.

I like the Christ-mas trees in shops a - long the way;
Then on the win-dow sill some can-dles there will be,

I like the best of all the things we give a - way.
Shin - ing on Christ-mas Eve for ev - 'ry-one to see.

O Come, Little Children

Translated

J. A. P. Schulz

Gently

1. O come, lit - tle chil - dren, O come, one and all,
2. O see, in the man - ger, in hal - low - ed light,

To Beth - le-hem's sta - ble, in Beth - le-hem's stall,
A star throws its beam on this ho - li - est sight.

And see with re - joic - ing this glo - ri - ous sight,
In clean swad-dling clothes lies the Heav - en - ly Child,

Our Fa - ther in Heav - en has sent us this night.
More love - ly than an - gels this Ba - by so mild.

What sweeter music can we bring
Than a carol for to sing.

Robert Herrick

O Come, All Ye Faithful

F. Oakeley

Old Latin

Steadily

O come, all ye faithful, Joyful and triumphant,
O come ye, O come ye to Bethlehem;
Come and behold Him, Born the King of Angels;
O come, let us adore Him,
O come, let us adore Him,
O come, let us adore Him,
Christ the Lord.

Away in a Manger

Traditional

Lightly

Away in a manger, no crib for His bed,
The little Lord Jesus laid down His sweet head.
The stars in the sky looked down where He lay,
The little Lord Jesus, asleep in the hay.

The cattle are lowing, the Baby awakes,
But little Lord Jesus, no crying He makes.
I love Thee, Lord Jesus, look down from the sky,
And stay by my cradle till morning is nigh.

O Little Town of Bethlehem

Phillips Brooks   Lewis H. Redner

Smoothly

O little town of Bethlehem,
How still we see thee lie,
Above thy deep and dreamless sleep
The silent stars go by;
Yet in thy dark streets shineth
The everlasting light,
The hopes and fears of all the years
Are met in thee tonight.

Silent Night

Joseph Mohr   Franz Grüber

Softly

Silent night, holy night!
All is calm, all is bright
Round yon Virgin Mother and Child.
Holy Infant so tender and mild,
Sleep in heavenly peace,
Sleep in heavenly peace.

We Wish You a Merry Christmas

Cornish Carol

Joyfully

We   wish   you   a   Mer-ry   Christ-mas,

We   wish   you   a   Mer-ry   Christ-mas,

We   wish   you   a   Mer-ry   Christ-mas,

And   a   Hap - py   New   Year.

Good ti - dings we bring

To you and your kin;

We wish you a Mer-ry Christ-mas,

And a Hap - py New Year.

A Jolly Party

Agnes Bell

Let's have a jol-ly par-ty, a par-ty, a par-ty.

Let's have a jol-ly par-ty on Val-en-tine's Day!

Val-en-tines for ev-'ry-one,

Games to play and lots of fun,

Let's have a jol-ly par-ty on Val-en-tine's Day!

A Special Valentine

Ena B. Knippel

Smoothly

Take a big red heart and a lit - tle piece of lace,

Draw a pret - ty flow'r with a hap - py, smil - ing face.

Wrap it all with love, And send it on its way.

It's a val - en - tine for moth - er on this spe - cial day.

Where do you find this pattern in the song?

so	fa	mi	re	do
5	4	3	2	1

Beautiful Bells at Easter Time

Smoothly

Naomi Caldwell

Beau - ti - ful bells, oh, hear their chime,

Beau - ti - ful bells at East - er time.

Ding dong, ding dong,

Ding dong, ding dong.

Beau - ti - ful bells, oh, hear their chime,

Beau - ti - ful bells at East - er time.

Play this music on the bells.

When the Easter bells sing, "Ding, dong," their music is *loud*. The sign for loud is *f*. When you hear their echo, the music is *soft*. The sign for soft is *p*.

108

At Easter Time

Laura E. Richards

Ethel Anthony

Brightly

1. The lit - tle flow'rs came thro' the ground
2. The pure white lil - y raised its cup

At East - er time, at East - er time;
At East - er time, at East - er time;

They raised their heads and looked a - round
The cro - cus to the sky looked up

At hap - py East - er time.
At hap - py East - er time.

This scalewise melody begins on *so*. Where do you find it in the song?

so	la	ti	do	re	mi	fa	so
5	6	7	8(1)	2	3	4	5

109

I Like to Make Up Songs

It is fun to make up or *compose* your own songs. When you compose a song, it is often better to start with a poem that is already written. Choose a poem you know or find a new poem you like. Read it to yourself many times. Try to feel the rhythm of the words. If it makes you think of musical sounds, you may be ready to write a melody for it.

Here is a short poem. You may compose a melody for it. First try to "say" or chant the words in rhythm.

> Bell horses, bell horses,
> What time of day?
> One o'clock, two o'clock,
> Three, and away.

Did you chant it this way?

or did you think of this rhythm?

Copy the words and music on the chalkboard just as they are at the bottom of the page. Be sure to put the words under the empty measures at the end where you will write your part of the melody.

Bell Horses

110

Sing the song as far as the melody goes in the book, then stop. Do not make a sound, but think how you would like to end the song. Sing the song again and end it, everyone singing his own way to make a good ending. You may have many different endings which are good. Perhaps you would like to sing your own idea for the ending of the melody while the others listen. Write some of the good endings on the chalkboard. Choose the one which you like the best. Sing the whole song in a quick, lively tempo.

Poems can have more than one rhythm and *meter*. The Bell Horses could trot or they could gallop. Here is another melody for you to complete. The pitches of the melody are the same, but the rhythm and the meter are different. Copy this song on the chalkboard and compose a good ending for it.

Bell Horses

Bell hors - es, bell hors - es, What time of day?

One o' - clock, two o' - clock, Three, and a - way.

After you have completed both songs, you may find that you like one better than the other. Write it down neatly.

Early to bed and early to rise
Makes a man healthy, wealthy, and wise.

This poem is said to have been written by Benjamin Franklin. It is good advice, isn't it? Say it over and over and feel the rhythm. Find the strong beats or *accents*.

Copy the song on the chalkboard just as it is in the book. This time you may compose all of the second line of the melody. (If you need some help, here is an idea. The first two measures of the second line may be like the first two measures of the first line.)

Early to Bed

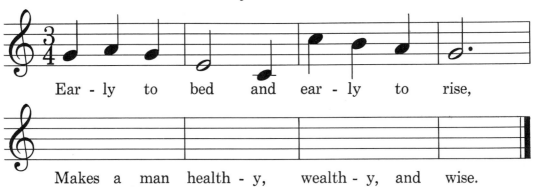

Ear - ly   to   bed   and   ear - ly   to   rise,

Makes   a   man   health - y,   wealth - y,   and   wise.

Here is another melody to complete. The words are the same, but the melody and the rhythm are different.

Early to Bed

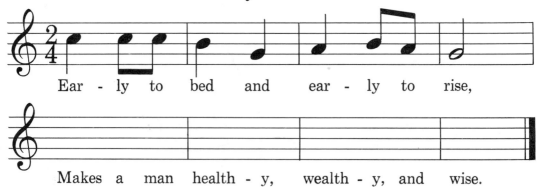

Ear - ly   to   bed   and   ear - ly   to   rise,

Makes   a   man   health - y,   wealth - y,   and   wise.

Do you like this rhythm better? Be sure to write down your songs as you compose them. Which one do you prefer? Why?

Music of Home and Country

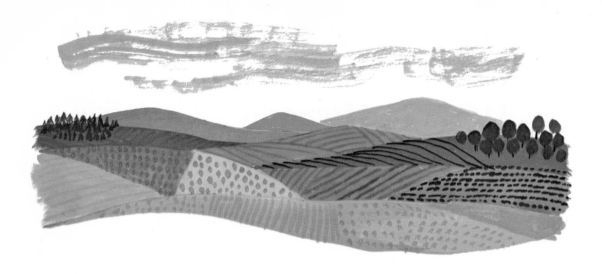

America, the Beautiful

Katharine Lee Bates

Samuel A. Ward

Majestically

O beau - ti - ful for spa-cious skies, For am-ber waves of grain,

For pur-ple moun-tain maj - es-ties A - bove the fruit-ed plain!

A - mer - i - ca! A - mer - i - ca! God shed His grace on thee,

And crown thy good with broth-er-hood From sea to shin-ing sea!

114

America

Samuel Francis Smith

Traditional

Proudly

My coun - try, 'tis of thee,

Sweet land of lib - er - ty,

Of thee I sing.

Land where my fa - thers died!

Land of the Pil - grims' pride!

From ev - 'ry_mountain-side, Let_ free - dom ring!

The home tone is G. On what tone does the song begin? On what tone does it end?

The Star-Spangled Banner

Francis Scott Key

John Stafford Smith

With spirit

O___ say! can you see, by the dawn's ear-ly light,

What so proud - ly we hail'd at the twi-light's last gleam-ing?

Whose broad stripes and bright stars, thro' the per - il - ous fight,

O'er the ram-parts we watch'd, were so gal-lant-ly stream-ing?

And the rock-ets' red glare, the bombs burst-ing in air,

Gave proof thro' the night that our flag was still there.

O say, does that Star-Span-gled Ban-ner yet wave

O'er the land ___ of the free and the home of the brave?

Yankee Doodle

Traditional

In marching tempo

Yan-kee Doo-dle came to town A - rid -ing on a po - ny,

He stuck a feath-er in his hat And called it mac-a - ro - ni.

Yan-kee Doo-dle keep it up, Yan-kee Doo-dle Dan - dy,

Mind the mu-sic and the step, And with the girls be hand - y.

Play a marching rhythm on the drum as you sing.

118

Our Flag

Norma VanZee

In moderate tempo

This   is   our flag;   red, white, and blue!

Be - fore   it   we stand proud - ly and true,

I pledge allegiance to the flag
of the United States of America
and to the republic for which it stands,
one nation under God, indivisible,
with liberty and justice for all.

Daddy's Lullaby

Dennis Krohn

Quietly

Go, go to your dad-dy, Hur-ry on home to him.

The sheep no more are roam-ing,

The birds are a-sleep on the limb.

So go, go to your dad-dy,

Hur-ry on home to him.

slower

Hur-ry on home, Hur-ry on home.

The repeat sign (:||) at the end of the first line
tells you to sing the line once again.

Sleep, Baby, Sleep!
(Schlaf, Kindchen, Schlaf!)

German Cradle Song

Gently

1. Sleep, ba - by, sleep! Thy fa - ther guards the sheep,
Schlaf, Kind-chen, schlaf!

Thy moth - er shakes the dream-land tree,

And from it fall sweet dreams for thee.

Sleep, ba - by, sleep!   Sleep, ba - by, sleep!
Schlaf, Kind-chen, schlaf!   *Schlaf, Kind-chen, schlaf!*

2. Sleep, baby, sleep!
The big stars are the sheep;
The wee stars are the lambs, I guess,
The fair moon is the shepherdess.
Sleep, baby, sleep! Sleep, baby, sleep!

Pronounce: *Shlahf, kindt-chyen, shlahf.*

Play this pattern on the bells when-ever you see it in the music. Can you play all the notes in the song?

On tip-toe comes the gentle dark
To help the children sleep
And silently, in silver paths,
The slumber fairies creep.

Dorothy Mason Pierce

Sing the home tone.
Can you sing the starting tone?

Dearest Child
(Niño Querido)

Spanish Folk Song

Tenderly

1. Sleep now, my   ba   -   by,   sleep now, my   dear;
   Ni - ño que - ri   -   do,   duér - me - te   ya,

Moth - er will sing as the night-time draws near.
Que mien-tras tan - to te can - ta ma - má.

2. Now little birds lie safe in their nest;
   They will have food when they wake from their rest.

   Los pajarillos duermen tambien
   Mientras sus padres buscan de comer.

   It's fun to sing in Spanish.

My Mother

Barbara Young

Carlton Beck

Tenderly

I like the way my moth - er talks,

I like the way she laughs and sings,

And oh, I like the way, the way she walks,

As if her feet had kind of wings. —

Can you make your voice sound as if you are singing to someone dear to you? After you learn this beautiful song, you may wish to sing it at home.

The Slumber Boat

Jessie L. Gaynor

Gently swinging

Ba-by's boat, the sil-ver moon, Sail-ing thro' the sky;—

Sail-ing o'er the sea of sleep While the clouds float by.—

Sail, ba-by, sail Out up-on the sea,—

On-ly don't for-get to sail Back a-gain to me.—

This American lullaby has been loved for many years. As you sing,
sway to the rhythm of the slumber boat. The gentle rocking motion
of the song comes from this rhythm pattern.

124

Indian Lullaby

Henry W. Longfellow   Walter H. Aiken

Gently
p

1. Rock-a-bye, my   lit-tle owl-et,   In the moss-y, sway-ing nest,
2. Hush-a-bye, my   lit-tle owl-et,   Man-y voic-es   sing to thee,

With thy lit-tle wood-land broth-ers, Close thine eyes and take thy rest.
"Hush-a-bye," the wa-ter whis-pers, "Hush!" re-plies the   tall pine tree.

pp

To   whoo,   to   whoo,   to   whoo,   to   whoo.

An owlet is a baby owl. His call is very soft in the quiet night. The sign for *very soft* is *pp*. How softly and beautifully can you sing the baby owl's call?

pp

To   whoo
D   G

125

Play the home tone on the bells or piano. Can you sing the starting tone? Try to sing this whole song by reading the notes.

Little Bird on My Window

Edith Krohner

German Folk Melody

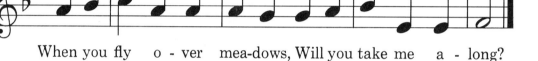

1. Lit-tle bird on my win-dow, Will you sing me a song?

When you fly o - ver mea-dows, Will you take me a - long?

2. There are beautiful flowers
   I can see from my door,
   But if I could go flying,
   I would see many more.

3. So come back to my window,
   Let your song never end.
   I will tell you a secret,
   You're a very good friend.

My Wish

Georgia Deal   Marian Major

Sprightly

My tooth came out and I put it   Just where my sis-ter said,

Un-der-neath my   pil - low,   Right be-low my   head.

And then, she said, I would get   my wish,

And that must have been the   truth,

For now   I have what I wished for,   A brand new   tooth.

I wake up in the morning early,
And always the very first thing,
I poke out my head
And I sit up in bed
And I sing and I sing and I sing!

Rose Fyleman

The Wake-Up Clock

Graham Haswell

Steadily

All night long I tick, tick, tick So soft - ly no one hears,

But soon the night-time goes a - way And day-time light ap-pears.

'Tis then I ring my wake-up song So ev - 'ry-bod - y hears.

I ring ding-a-ling, ding-a-ling, ling, ling, Wake up, wake up, my dears!

You can play this song on the bells.
Which instrument can make the "tick-tick" sound?
Which instrument can make the "ding-a-ling" sound?
When should you play these instruments?

128

Tommy

Georgia Deal

Duncan Ross

With spirit

1. Tom-my is a space - man, Tom-my is a gro - cer,
2. Tom-my is a cow - boy, Tom-my is a band, —

Tom-my is a die - sel train, or a roll - er coast-er.
Tom-my is an air - plane just a-bout to land. —

3. Tom-my is a sol - dier, rid-ing in a jeep, —

slower

When Tom-my is just Tom - my, that's when he's a - sleep!

This repeat sign (:∥) tells you to go back to the beginning and sing the second verse.

What does this sign (⌢) tell you to do?

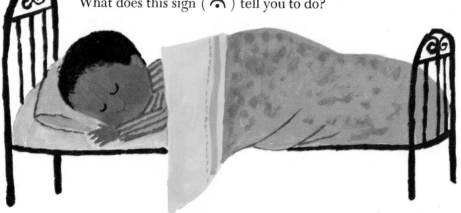

129

My Donkey

E. M. E.

Portuguese Folk Melody

Rhythmically

1. I wish that I had   a don-key, I'd ride on him ev - 'ry - day;
2. I'd ride him to school each morn-ing And home at the end of day;

I'd pat him and call him Pe - dro And feed him on oats and hay.
And all of my friends could ride him As we went a - long the way.

When you know this song, make up your own autoharp accompaniment. Begin with the F major chord.

Choose an instrument to play a "clip-clop" rhythm.

What is the home tone of this song?

Little Chick

Alice Ricky

Dolores Batres G.

Lightly

1. Lit-tle fluf-fy chick so yel-low   Com-ing from a lit-tle shell,
2. All the chick-ens in the farm-yard, Show their feath-ers off to you,

Look-ing like a pet ca-na-ry,   Sing-ing like a lit-tle bell.
When you are a grown-up chick-en, You'll have chick-en feath-ers too.

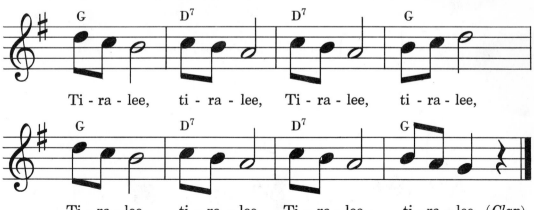

Ti - ra - lee,   ti - ra - lee,   Ti - ra - lee,   ti - ra - lee,

Ti - ra - lee,   ti - ra - lee,   Ti - ra - lee,   ti - ra - lee. (*Clap*)

Hideaway Bunny

Barbara Heath

Francis J. Pyle

With a bounce

1. Lit - tle Bun - ny   Rab - bit went hop - ping one   day,
2. Lit - tle Bun - ny   Rab - bit took fright at   a   sound,

Look - ing for his break - fast a - long the   way.—
Quick - ly he went rac - ing a - cross the   ground,

He came in - to our gar - den and nib - bled leaves of green.
And we could nev - er find him to say, "Come back and play."

He thought he'd have a sal - ad, and not   be   seen.
I   guess he hid him - self   in his hide - a - way.

The wood block will sound like a hopping bunny if you play this rhythm.

Music for Fun

The Hen Who Quacked

Naomi Caldwell

Not too fast

Once there was a lit - tle hen who thought she'd be a duck.

She got up in the morn-ing and said, "quack" in-stead of "cluck."

But when she saw the ducks were in the pond be-yond the wall,

"Cluck cluck," she cried, "I can-not swim, I'm a chick-en af - ter all.

Cluck cluck, cluck cluck, I'm a chick-en af - ter all."

Six Little Ducks

Gaily

Folk Song

1. Six lit - tle ducks that I once knew,

Fat ones skin - ny ones, fair ones, too.

REFRAIN

But the one lit - tle duck with a feath - er in his back,

He led the oth - ers with a quack, quack, quack,

Quack, quack, quack, quack, quack, quack,

He led the oth - ers with a quack, quack, quack.

2. Down to the river they would go,
   Wibble, wobble, wibble, wobble,
   to and fro. (*Refrain*)

3. Home from the river they would come,
   Wibble, wobble, wibble, wobble,
   ho hum hum. (*Refrain*)

The House of the Mouse

Lucy Sprague Mitchell

Barbara Heath

Lively

The house of the mouse is a wee lit-tle house,

A green lit-tle house in the grass,

Which big clum-sy folk may hunt and may poke

And still nev-er see as they pass

This sweet lit-tle, neat lit-tle, wee lit-tle, green lit-tle,

Cud-dle-down hide-a-way house in the grass.

PUPIL ANNOUNCER. Hello, everybody! Our class now brings you "Music Time" over station _____ –TV. Everyone knows that this is the happiest time of the day, so let's all sing together, because it's "Music Time" again.

It's Music Time Again

Marian Major

It's mu - sic time a - gain,— Mu - sic time a - gain.

So join in the song and go sing - ing a - long,

For it's mu - sic time a - gain!—

First on our program today will be a dance by—guess who—our dancing puppets. We will all sing while the puppets dance. [*Several children may be the puppets.*]

The Puppet Show

Katherine S. Bolt — Old Dutch Melody

1. We are lit - tle danc - ing pup - pets,
Daf - fa - dil - ly, Daf-fa-down dil - ly,
We are lit - tle danc - ing pup - pets,
Daf-fa-down dil - ly - o.

2. We can nod our heads to greet you, Daffadilly, etc.
3. We can clap our hands together, Daffadilly, etc.
4. We can bow and we can curtsy, Daffadilly, etc.
5. We can wave good-by and leave you, Daffadilly, etc.

ANNOUNCER. Thank you, puppets. They were ___(pupils'___
___names)___ . The next song will be sung by the girls. It is a
song about Amelia. Do you know her? Have you ever seen
her?

I Know Amelia

Katherine S. Bolt   Portuguese Folk Song

1. I know A - me - lia, she is so small

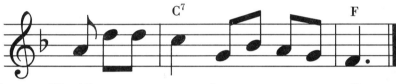

You'll nev-er see her, no, not at all.

2. I saw Amelia right by my plate.
   A little bread crumb was all she ate.

3. I saw Amelia quick as a wink
   Slide down the soap and into the sink.

4. I saw Amelia tucked in her bed,
   One pussywillow beneath her head.

5. I know Amelia, she is my friend,
   She's always with me when I pretend.

ANNOUNCER. Thank you, girls. Boys, are you ready for
that lively Indian dance? ___(Pupil's name)___ will play
the Indian drum. The girls will sing while the boys dance.

Dance, Indian Man

Steve Corcoran

Rhythmically and rather fast

1, 2. Dance, dance, dance, dance, In - di - an man.

1. Shake your rat - tle, beat your drum, Oh, it must be lots of fun.
2. Stamp your foot up - on the ground, Turn your bod - y all a - round.

Dance, dance, dance, dance, In - di - an man.

Ah ha, Ah ha.

ANNOUNCER. Wasn't that an exciting dance! Thank you, boys. And now our closing feature will be the "Riddle Song." Our soloists are ___(pupils' names)___ . Be ready to guess the riddles!

["Riddle Song" *may be sung by three soloists, one for each verse. Play the piano accompaniment once after each verse while the singer or another pupil acts out the motions of the animal. The* ANNOUNCER *asks, "What is it?" and the audience guesses the answer before going to the next verse.*]

Riddle Song

Agnes Bell

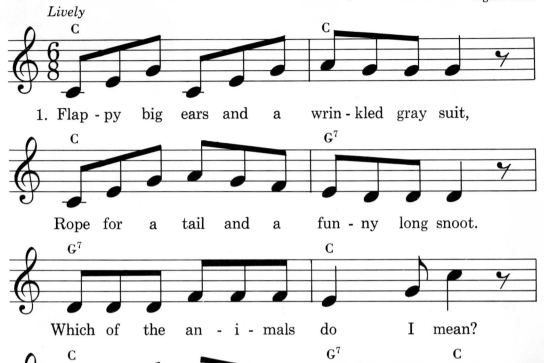

Lively

1. Flap - py big ears and a wrin - kled gray suit,

Rope for a tail and a fun - ny long snoot.

Which of the an - i - mals do I mean?

Just guess the larg - est you ev - er have seen.

2. There is an animal kept in a cage,
   Often he's growling and roaring in rage.
   Beautiful mane and a smooth brown coat,
   Which of the animals now gets your vote?

3. There is a creature who lives in the sea,
   Flippers for feet, and some whiskers has he.
   Funniest bark you have ever heard,
   Now can you guess it with only one word?

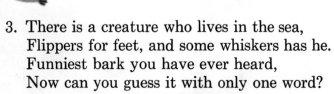

141

ANNOUNCER. We hope all of you have enjoyed our program of fun songs. Tune in again to "Music Time," which was brought to you by Room _____ of _____ School. Our producer and director was ___(teacher's name)___. And now here is our theme song, "It's Music Time Again."

It's Music Time Again

Marian Major

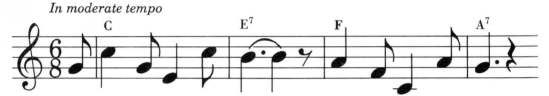

It's mu - sic time a - gain,___ Mu - sic time a - gain.

So join in the song and go sing - ing a - long,

For it's mu - sic time a - gain!___

Fun with Instruments

Many melodies have been written just for instruments. They do not have any words. They may be played by a big band or an orchestra, by a smaller group of instruments, or by a solo instrument.

Here are some melodies for you to play on the bells or on the piano. You may wish to play an accompaniment on the autoharp too. Can you make these two pieces sound like the big chimes in the steeple of a church?

Westminster Chimes

Norfolk Chimes

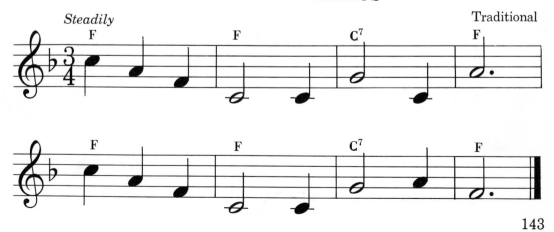

Musette

Lightly

Johann Sebastian Bach

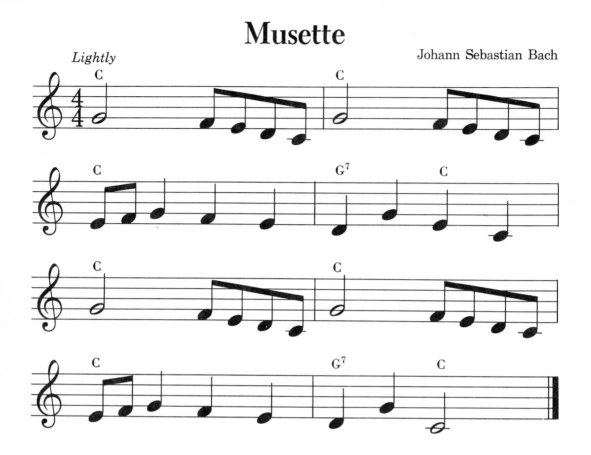

Très Jolie Waltz

Gracefully

Emil Waldteufel

Pronounce: *Tray zhoh-lee.*

Pretend that you are skating to this lovely waltz. Can you make sand blocks sound like your skates on the ice?

Debka Hora

Palestinian Folk Dance

Lively

The *hora* is a folk dance for everyone to do together in a big circle.

Magic Bell Song

From *The Magic Flute*
Wolfgang Amadeus Mozart

Happily

In the story of *The Magic Flute*, the magic bells have the power to protect the Prince and his friend, Papageno, from danger and harm while they are looking for the Princess.

145

Here are some more melodies for you to play, but you will need to complete them. Copy the first part of the song on the chalkboard, then play it and write an ending for it. There may be more than one good ending for each song.

Perhaps you have a whole melody singing in your mind. Be sure to write it down so you won't forget it. Just think how many different melodies you can make up and play!

Music from Tip to Toe

How Do You Do Today?

Carol Davis   Italian Folk Melody

Happily

Bright and ear - ly in the morn - ing

When you go a - long your way,

Hap - py smiles will sure - ly greet you

If to ev - 'ry - one you say:

"Oh, how do you do to - day?

Oh, how do you do to - day?

Oh, how do you do to - day, my friend,

Oh, how do you do to - day?"

In which part of the song do you shake hands with your neighbors?

Dance, My Top!

Adapted by E. M. E.

French-Canadian Folk Song

Oh, lit - tle top, will you dance for me?

Oh, lit - tle top, will you dance for me?

A bright {red blue green} ring you will have, you see!

A bright {red blue green} ring you will have, you see!

Dance, my top, oh dance now,

And hum to me so sweet - ly,

Your col - ors spar - kle, so bright and clear,

Oh, lit - tle top, will you dance right here!

The song for this game is easy to learn because so many lines of the melody are exactly alike. Where do you find them?

Choose one pupil to be the top. Form a circle and dance around him. At line five of the song, stop and watch the top make some kind of little dance or motion. At line seven everyone tries to copy the same motion. At the end, the top chooses a new top from the circle and the game begins again.

151

Skip to My Lou

Lively

Traditional

1. Lost my part - ner, what will I do,

Lost my part - ner, what will I do,

Lost my part - ner, what will I do?

Skip to my Lou, my dar - ling.

Skip, skip, skip to my Lou, Skip, skip, skip to my Lou,

Skip, skip, skip to my Lou, Skip to my Lou, my dar - ling.

2. I'll get another one, better than you, etc.
3. Can't get a red bird, a blue bird will do, etc.
4. Little red wagon, painted blue, etc.
5. Fly in the sugar bowl, shoo, shoo, shoo, etc.

The notes of this melody make two chords.

The Bus

In moderate tempo

1. The peo-ple on the bus go up and down,
2. The wheels on the bus go round and round,

Up and down, up and down.
Round and round, round and round.

The peo-ple on the bus go up and down,
The wheels on the bus go round and round,

All through the town.
All through the town.

3. The horn on the bus goes too, too, too, etc.

4. The money in the box goes ding, ding, ding, etc.

5. The wiper on the glass goes swish, swish, swish, etc.

153

Jingle at the Windows

Moderately fast

Traditional Singing Game

Pass one win - dow, ti - de - o,

Pass two win - dows, ti - de - o,

Pass three win - dows, ti - de - o,

Jin-gle at the win - dows, ti - de - o.

Ti - de - o, ti - de - o, Jin-gle at the win-dows, ti - de - o,

Ti - de - o, ti - de - o, Jin-gle at the win-dows, ti - de - o.

The home tone of this song is E flat (E♭).

Form a single circle of partners with left hands on the right shoulder of the person ahead. At line five, boys turn, lock right elbows, and swing with the girl behind. At line six, lock left elbows and swing.

154

Bake a Cherry Pie

Katherine S. Bolt

French Folk Melody

1. Bake a cher - ry pie, sing-ing ti - ra, li - ra, li - ra,
2. Roll the pie-crust thin, sing-ing ti - ra, li - ra, li - ra,

Bake a cher - ry pie, sing-ing ti - ra, li - ra, lo.
Roll the pie-crust thin, sing-ing ti - ra, li - ra, lo.

Pull your sleeves up high, sing-ing ti - ra, li - ra, li - ra,
Pour the sug - ar in, sing-ing ti - ra, li - ra, li - ra,

Pull your sleeves up high, sing-ing ti - ra, li - ra, lo.
Pour the sug - ar in, sing-ing ti - ra, li - ra, lo.

3. Put it in to cook, singing etc.
   Put it in to cook, singing etc.
   Now we'll take a look, singing etc.
   Now we'll take a look, singing etc.

4. Cut the pieces small, singing etc.
   Cut the pieces small, singing etc.
   There's enough for all, singing etc.
   There's enough for all, singing etc.

156

On the Bridge of Avignon
(Sur le Pont d'Avignon)

Stately   French Folk Song

On the bridge of   A - vi-gnon,   All are danc-ing, all are danc-ing;
Sur le pont ___ d'A-vi-gnon, L'on y dan-se, L'on y dan-se;

On the bridge of   A - vi-gnon,   All are danc-ing   in   a   ring.
Sur le pont ___ d'A-vi-gnon, L'on y dan-se   tout en rond.

1. Gen-tle-men bow this   way, Then a-gain bow that   way.
2. La-dies curt-sy   this   way, Then they curt-sy that   way.

Pronounce: *Syuhr luh pohn dah-vee-nyohn, loh-nee dawn-suh, loh-nee dawn-suh;*
Syuhr luh pohn dah-vee-nyohn, loh-nee dawn-suh toot awn rohn.

Make up your own little dance for this old French folk song.

D.C. tells you to go back to the beginning of the song. After you
have sung the last verse, go back to the beginning once more and
sing until you come to the word *Fine* (pronounced *fee-nay*). This
is the end of the song.

To Paree
(A Paris)

French Folk Song

In trotting tempo

1. To Pa - ree, to Pa - ree, Po - ny gray will car - ry me.
   A Pa - ris, à Pa - ris, Sur un pe - tit che -val gris.

2. To Verdun, to Verdun
   On a little pony brown.

   A Verdun, à Verdun,
   Sur un petit cheval brun.

3. To Cambrai, to Cambrai,
   On a little pony bay.

   A Cambrai, à Cambrai,
   Sur un petit cheval bai.

4. Now come back, now come back,
   On a little pony black.

   Revenons au manoir
   Sur un petit cheval noir.

Pronounce: 1. *Ah Pah-ree, ah Pah-ree,*
Syuhr uhn puh-tee shuh-vahl gree.
4. *Ruh-vuh-nohn oh mah-nwahr,* etc.

This little song has only four different tones. Can you read it by yourself? Add a "clip-clop" accompaniment with a wood block or coconut shells.

Seesaw

Judith M. Berman

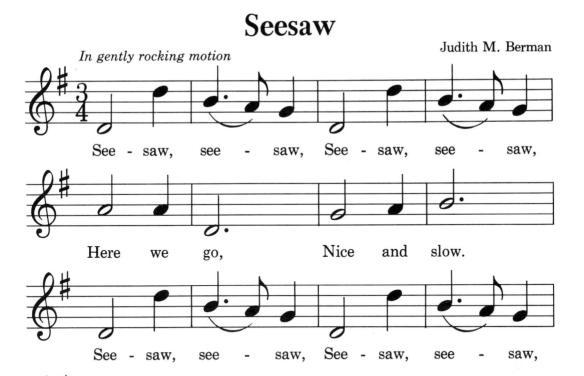

In gently rocking motion

See - saw, see - saw, See - saw, see - saw,

Here we go, Nice and slow.

See - saw, see - saw, See - saw, see - saw,

Sail - ing down, Then up we go.

How many times is this pattern used in this song? Name the tones.
Find the octave.

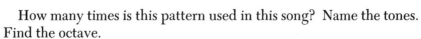

The Allee Allee O

Folk Song from Massachusetts

Oh, the big ship's a-sail-ing through the Al-lee Al-lee O,

The Al-lee Al-lee O, The Al-lee Al-lee O.

Oh, the big ship's a-sail-ing through the Al-lee Al-lee O,

Hi! Ding-dong day!

160

Little Old Tugboat

Joseph Gerard

Steadily

Lit-tle old tug - boat works on the riv - er,

Lit-tle old tug - boat works on the bay;

Push-es the big ships up the riv - er,

Push-es the barg - es out of the way.

"Toot, toot, toot!" hear him com-ing,

Down the riv - er, down the bay.

Sing the home tone and the starting tone. Which lines begin differently from the first line? Play a steady "chug-chug" accompaniment on sand blocks.

Chiapanecas

Mexican Folk-Dance Song

Rhythmically

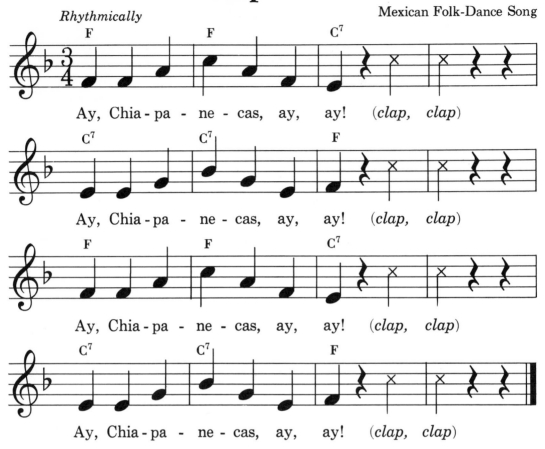

Ay, Chia-pa - ne - cas, ay, ay! (*clap, clap*)

Ay, Chia-pa - ne - cas, ay, ay! (*clap, clap*)

Ay, Chia-pa - ne - cas, ay, ay! (*clap, clap*)

Ay, Chia-pa - ne - cas, ay, ay! (*clap, clap*)

Pronounce: *Chyah-pah-nay-kas*

162

Rain-Dance Song

M. M. *In moderate tempo*   Zuñi Indian

1. Come a-gain,   come a-gain,   come,   good rain,
2. Come a-gain,   come a-gain,   come,   good rain,

Fall up-on the moun-tains   and   on   the   plain.
Wa-ter for the riv-ers   and   for   the   grain.

Can you make up a rain dance for this song? Play an accompaniment while you sing and dance.

Big Drum and Little Drum

Dorothy Scott

In marching tempo

Big Drum speaks and Lit-tle Drum lis - tens,

Big Drum speaks and Lit-tle Drum hears.

Lit-tle Drum speaks and Big Drum lis - tens,

Lit-tle Drum speaks and Big Drum hears.

Big Drum speaks and Lit - tle Drum lis - tens,

Big Drum speaks and Lit - tle Drum hears.

Big Drum

Tap the rhythm of the parts written for the big drum and little drum. How is the sound of the big drum different from the sound of the little drum?

The Drum Major

Jane Tinsley

Barbara Heath

Proudly

1,2. I am a tall drum ma-jor,

1. In my boots and gold-en braid.
2. I am lead-ing the pa - rade.

See my white fur cap and my coat of red.
Keep-ing step, hep, hep, to the march-ing band,

See my shin-ing stick as I march a-head.
Step-ping high, so high, to the mu - sic grand.

I'm the lead-er of the pa-rade,

I'm the lead-er of the pa-rade.

DANCE -A- STORY

with **ANNE LIEF BARLIN**…about

The Magic Mountain

Written by **PAUL** and **ANNE BARLIN**
Illustrations by **LOIS ZENER THOMAS**

Have you ever been on a horse? Do you know that you can ride sideways or even backwards? See how many different ways you can ride when you hear the music galloping. You can even *be* the horse, lifting your knees very high as horses do when they gallop.

This is a "pretending" story. If you want to, you can be a horse and then a rider and change whenever you like! And *then* when you get to the top of "The Magic Mountain" you can turn into a bird or a tree or even into the wind! Many wonderful things happen to you on this mountain. Hurry now, so that you can "Dance-A-Story about The Magic Mountain."

Anne Lief Barlin

"Dance-A-Story about The Magic Mountain," with music and narration, is available on RCA Victor long-play record LE–103 and may be purchased through Ginn and Company.

Let's get on a
horse for a
trip to the
mountain

Giddy-ap, qiddy-ap, qiddy-ap, qiddy-ap
And ride and ride and ride and ride
Giddy-ap, qiddy-ap . . .

...now gallop and gallop
Sit straight in the saddle
and ride

The road winds to the left...

And now to the right

Then

it goes up...

174

And now it goes
down...

Here comes a tunnel
Get all the way down

Are you scared
in the dark ?

Out in the sunshine
once again and you
ride, ride,
ride, ride

178

Up ... up ...
clear to the top !

And you stop

Whoa !

You sit up straight
and look around

There's something
strange about
the air up here...

You get off
your horse . . .

and tie him up

You see a bird
fly overhead

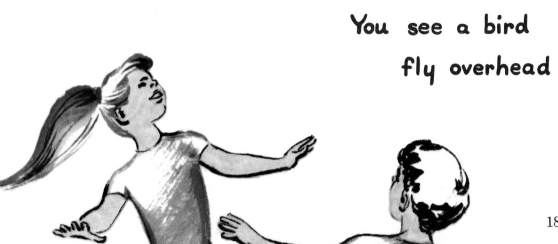

You watch
him swoop...

You watch
him glide...

You watch...
You watch...
He soars up high

You watch...
You watch...
Now <u>you</u> want to fly !

(This is the magic of
this special mountain.
You turn into
everything you see.)

There is a tree
Some of its branches
are high...
And some are low...

The branches sway
And the leaves rustle
When the wind blows

191

A leaf
falls from
a branch...

192

...and starts a
slow, turning, twisting glide
to earth

The wind blows
it this way

and that way

and turns it

around...

Finally it settles . . .

down to the ground

And now <u>you</u> are
the wind

You blow

forward

and back...

forward
and back

...and side

...to side

High over the
tops of the trees

Blow the wildflowers
low on the ground

Nothing can stop you
You twirl round
and around

199

And now it is night
It suddenly turns cold

Something is floating
   from the sky...
You're a snowflake
Falling gently
Turning softly
Snowing, snowing
All the night...

When the morning
comes, you hear many
happy voices...
(Oh look, oh look, oh look
at the snow! Yay! Yay!)
The children have come
to play in the snow

You are the children

You make snowballs
to throw

You throw
and duck

and throw
and duck...

and throw and duck
and throw and duck

Let's build a snowman...
Make him big
Oh, very big !

Build him round
And build him fat
All the way
round...
Pat, pat

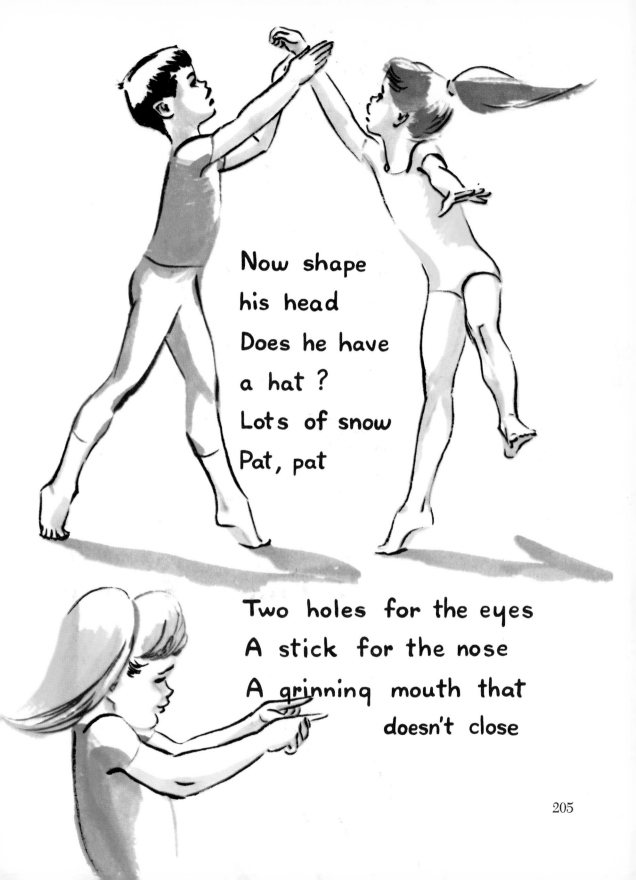

Now shape
his head
Does he have
a hat ?
Lots of snow
Pat, pat

Two holes for the eyes
A stick for the nose
A grinning mouth that
doesn't close

205

But the
mountain
is
magic...

and... you...
turn...
into...
the...
snowman

A snowman
so funny!

You can't
move!

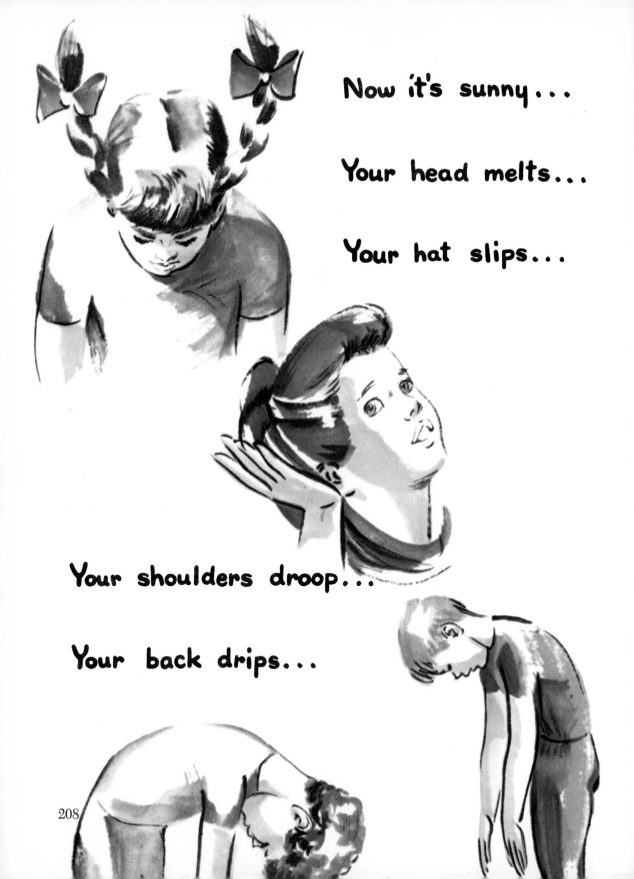

Now it's sunny...

Your head melts...

Your hat slips...

Your shoulders droop...

Your back drips...

208

Your arms melt...

Your knees bend down...

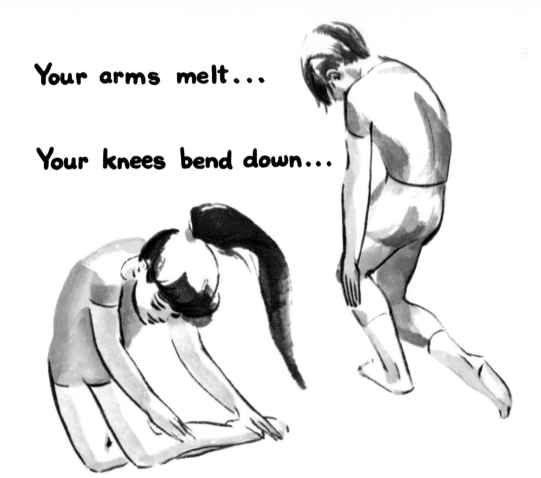

You melt to a puddle
Just water
on
the
ground

210

The puddle rolls and rolls
into a stream ...
It's rushing and rolling down
    the mountain
You've come to the bottom ...

The magic is gone
You turn into yourself

Jump up !
Look around...
Who has followed
you all the way
down ?

Your faithful horse...

Up in the saddle...

...and gallop on home.

Classified Index

ACTION SONGS AND GAMES

Bake a Cherry Pie 156
Big Drum and Little Drum 164
Bus, The 153
Dance, Indian Man 140
Dance, My Top! 150
Jingle at the Windows 154
Puppet Show, The 138
Skip to My Lou 152

ANIMALS

Bambi (Song Story) 65
Hideaway Bunny 132
House of the Mouse, The 136
My Donkey 130
Riddle Song 141
To Paree 158

AUTOHARP ACCOMPANIMENTS

Two Chords
Bake a Cherry Pie 156
Chiapanecas 162
Dance, My Top! 150
Hen Who Quacked, The 134
I Know Amelia 139
I Like to Sing 7
Little Chick 131
Musette 144
Norfolk Chimes 143
Puppet Show, The 138
Riddle Song 141
Six Little Ducks 135
Skip to My Lou 152
Sleep, Baby, Sleep! 121

Three Chords
Christmastime 100
Dearest Child 122
Debka Hora 145

Happy Birthday to You 85
How Do You Do Today? 148
Little Man in the Wood 64
Magic Bell Song 145
Pumpkin Face 88
Spring Magic 58
Stand Up! 84
Thanksgiving Day 90

More Than Three Chords
Allee Allee O, The 160
It's Music Time Again 137, 142
Little Bird on My Window 126
Little Sir Echo 50
Now It Is Yule 96
Our Flag 119
Pick a Pumpkin 87
Très Jolie Waltz 144
Wind, The 56

BIRDS AND FOWL

Hen Who Quacked, The 134
Indian Lullaby 125
Little Bird on My Window 126
Little Chick 131
Nightingale, The 62
See the Little Ducklings 22
Six Little Ducks 135

BIRTHDAYS

Happy Birthday to You 85
Stand Up! 84

CHRISTMAS

Away in a Manger 102
Christmas Cradle Song 97
Christmastime 100
Elves' Christmas Eve, The 98
Merry Christmas! 97

Now It Is Yule 96
O Christmas Tree 94
O Come, All Ye Faithful 102
O Come, Little Children 101
O Little Town of Bethlehem 103
Silent Night 103
We Wish You a Merry Christmas . . . 104

CREATIVE EXPERIENCES

Bell Horses 110, 111
Early to Bed 112
Fun with Instruments 146
Have You Heard the Wind? 48
Magic Mountain, The (Dance-A-Story) 167
My Donkey 130
Wind, The 56

DANCES

Chiapanecas 162
Dance in a Circle 15
Dance, Indian Man 140
Debka Hora 145
Magic Mountain, The (Dance-A-Story) 167
On the Bridge of Avignon 157
Rain-Dance Song 163

DRAMATIZATION

Bambi (Song Story) 65
Elves' Christmas Eve, The 98
Hideaway Bunny 132
Little Sir Echo 50
Magic Mountain, The (Dance-A-Story) 167
March of the Little Flags 9
My Little Red Drum 10
Puppet Show, The 138
Riddle Song 141
Spring Magic 58
Tommy 129

EASTER

At Easter Time 109
Beautiful Bells at Easter Time 108

FOREIGN LANGUAGE

English Title
Christmas Cradle Song (*French*) . . . 97
Dearest Child (*Spanish*) 122
Merry Christmas! (*Spanish*) 97
Now It Is Yule (*Swedish*) 96
O Christmas Tree (*German*) 94
On the Bridge of Avignon (*French*) . 157
Sleep, Baby, Sleep! (*German*) 121
To Paree (*French*) 158

Foreign Language Title
A Paris (*French*) 158
¡Feliz Navidad! (*Spanish*) 97
Niño Querido (*Spanish*) 122
Nu Är Det Jul (*Swedish*) 96
O Tannenbaum (*German*) 94
Schlaf, Kindchen, Schlaf! (*German*) . 121
Sur le Pont d'Avignon (*French*) . . . 157

HALLOWEEN

Hurray for Halloween! 86
Pick a Pumpkin 87
Pumpkin Face 88

HANUKKAH

Candles Burning 92
Hanukkah Time 93

HOME AND FAMILY

After School 38
Bake a Cherry Pie 156
Daddy's Lullaby 120
Dearest Child 122
Early to Bed 112
Go to Sleep 36
Happy Birthday to You 85
If You Can't Say Something Nice . . . 70
My Mother 123
My Wish 127
Pumpkin Face 88
Rockabye Song, A 32

Sleep, Baby, Sleep! 121
Slumber Boat, The 124
Thank You 91
Tommy 129
Wake-Up Clock, The 128

INDIVIDUAL RESPONSE

April Day, An 57
Bell Horses 110, 111
Early to Bed 112
Fun with Instruments (Unit) 146
Little Sir Echo 50
My Little Red Drum 10
Wind, The 56

INSTRUMENTAL ENRICHMENT

Bells or Piano
Beautiful Bells at Easter Time 108
Bell Horses 110, 111
Debka Hora 145
Early to Bed. 112
Fun with Instruments 146
Happy Birthday to You 85
Have You Heard the Wind? 48
Little Bird on My Window 126
Magic Bell Song 145
Music We Can Sing and Play (Section) 19–42
Musette 144
Nightingale, The 62
Norfolk Chimes 143
Ring-ting-tingle 17
Sleep, Baby, Sleep! 121
Très Jolie Waltz 144
Wake-Up Clock, The 128
Westminster Chimes 143

Percussion Instruments
After School 38
Big Drum and Little Drum 164
Bye'm Bye 63
Dance, Indian Man 140
Drum Major, The 166
Happy Birthday to You 85
Little Old Tugboat 161

My Donkey 130
My Little Red Drum 10
Rain-Dance Song 163
Snowflakes 54
Stars 53
To Paree 158
Très Jolie Waltz 144
Wake-Up Clock, The 128
Yankee Doodle 118

LULLABIES AND QUIET MUSIC

Autumn Rainbow 46
Bye'm Bye 63
Christmas Cradle Song 97
Daddy's Lullaby 120
Dearest Child 122
Go to Sleep 36
Indian Lullaby 125
Moonlight 20, 34
Rockabye Song, A 32
Sleep, Baby, Sleep! 121
Slumber Bells 37
Slumber Boat, The 124
Snowflakes 54
Thank You 91

NATURE

America, the Beautiful 114
At Easter Time 109
Bambi (Song Story) 65
Bye'm Bye 63
Clouds 49
It's So Nice on the Ice 78
Little Man in the Wood 64
Moonlight 34
Snowflakes 54
Spring Magic 58
Stars 53
Twinkle, Twinkle, Little Star 26

NONSENSE

Hen Who Quacked, The 134
House of the Mouse, The 136

I Know Amelia 139
One, Two, Three 31
Riddle Song 141
Six Little Ducks 135

PATRIOTIC

America 115
America, the Beautiful 114
Our Flag 119
Star-Spangled Banner, The 116
Yankee Doodle 118

PRAISE AND THANKS

America 115
America, the Beautiful 114
Lights 52
Norfolk Chimes 143
Thank You 91
Thanksgiving 89
Thanksgiving Day 90
Westminster Chimes 143

RHYTHMIC ACTIVITIES

Clapping
Chiapanecas 162
Dance in a Circle 15
Little Chick 131
Puppet Show, The 138

Creative Movement
Allee Allee O, The 160
Autumn Rainbow 46
Balloons 60
Big Drum and Little Drum 164
Dance, Indian Man 140
Indian Lullaby 125
Leaf Kites 47
Little Chick 131
Little Wind 39
Puppet Show, The 138
Rain-Dance Song 163
Six Little Ducks 135
Snowflakes 54

Très Jolie Waltz 144

Galloping or Skipping
Dance in a Circle 15
How Do You Do Today? 148
Jolly Party, A 106
Puppet Show, The 138

Jumping or Hopping
Dance, Indian Man 140
Hideaway Bunny 132
Puppet Show, The 138

Marching or Walking
Big Drum and Little Drum 164
Drum Major, The 166
Jingle at the Windows 154
Jolly Party, A 106
Little Old Tugboat 161
March of the Little Flags 9
My Little Red Drum 10
Yankee Doodle 118

Running or Trotting
Allee Allee O, The 160
Dance, Indian Man 140
Elves' Christmas Eve, The 98
To Paree 158
Yankee Doodle 118

Swaying or Rocking
Chiapanecas 162
Daddy's Lullaby 120
Dearest Child 122
Go to Sleep 36
Here We Go Skating 29
Indian Lullaby 125
It's So Nice on the Ice 78
Little Old Tugboat 161
Morning Bells 25
Rockabye Song, A 32
Seesaw 159
Sleep, Baby, Sleep! 121
Slumber Bells 37
Slumber Boat, The 124
Spring Song 66, 82

SEASONS AND WEATHER

April Day, An 57
Autumn 30
Autumn Rainbow 46
Have You Heard the Wind? 48
Leaf Kites 47
Little April Shower 75
Little Wind 39
Rain-Dance Song 163
Spring Magic 58
Spring Song 66, 82
Wind, The 56

SONG STORIES AND UNITS

Bambi (Song Story) 65
Fun with Instruments (Unit) 143

I Like to Make Up Songs (Unit) . . . 110
Magic Mountain, The (Dance-A-Story) 167
Magic of Musical Sound, The (Unit) . 44
Music Time (Unit) 137
Music We Can Sing and Play (Section) 19

THANKSGIVING

Thank You 91
Thanksgiving 89
Thanksgiving Day 90

VALENTINE'S DAY

Jolly Party, A 106
Special Valentine, A 107

My Music Dictionary

Accent. An accent is a strong beat. An accented word or note gets a little more "push" than others. (page 140)

Beat. Beats are the number of taps or counts in a measure. There are four beats in a $\frac{4}{4}$ measure. (page 37)

Chord. A chord is heard when three or more tones are sounded at the same time. (page 39)

D.C. stands for the Italian words *Da Capo* (pronounce: *dah kah-poh*). It means "from the head" or "from the top." It tells you to go back to the beginning of the song. (page 157)

Dynamics. Dynamic signs tell you how loudly or softly the music is to be played or sung. *p* stands for the Italian word *piano* (pronounce: *pee-ah-noh*). It means "soft" or "quiet." *f* stands for *forte* (pronounce: *for-tay*). It means "loud."

pp	very soft (page 125)
p	soft (page 108)
mp	medium soft (page 164)
mf	medium loud (page 164)
f	loud (page 108)
ff	very loud

Fine (pronounce: *fee-nay*). *Fine* means "the end" in Italian. It tells you where to stop if you have repeated part of the song. (page 157)

Hold. A hold sign over a note (⌢) or under a note (⌣) tells you to hold that note a little longer than usual. (page 58)

Home tone. The home tone is the tonal center of the song. It is called the keynote or "*do.*" (page 34)

Musical phrase. A musical phrase is a sentence of music. (page 38)

Notes. Notes are signs which stand for tones. Different kinds of notes tell you how long to sing or play each tone.

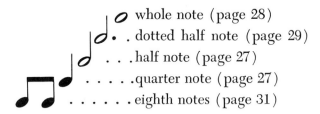

whole note (page 28)
dotted half note (page 29)
half note (page 27)
quarter note (page 27)
eighth notes (page 31)

Octave. An octave is the distance between the first and eighth tones of the scale. (page 48)

Pattern. A pattern is a short musical idea which is repeated. (page 57)

Repeat sign. Repeat signs look like: ‖ and ‖ ‖ . They show what part of the music is to be sung or played twice. (pages 62 and 120)

Rests. Rests are signs which tell you to be silent. Different kinds of rests tell you how long to be silent.

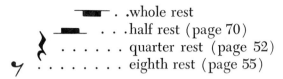

whole rest
half rest (page 70)
quarter rest (page 52)
eighth rest (page 55)

Scale. A scale is a series of tones which sounds like a musical "ladder." (page 24)

Tone. A tone is a single musical sound. (page 20)

Alphabetical Index

[All selections are recorded in Albums MM–2A, MM–2B, MM–2C, and MM–2D as designated.]

SELECTION	PAGE	ALBUM
After School	38	2A
Allee Allee O, The	160	2D
America	115	2C
America, the Beautiful	114	2C
April Day, An	57	2B
At Easter Time	109	2C
Autumn	30	2A
Autumn Rainbow	46	2A
Away in a Manger	102	2C
Bake a Cherry Pie	156	2D
Balloons	60	2B
Bambi (Song Story)	65	2B
Beautiful Bells at Easter Time	108	2C
Bell Horses	110	
Big Drum and Little Drum	164	2D
Bus, The	153	2D
Bye'm Bye	63	2B
Candles Burning	92	2B
Chiapanecas	162	2D
Christmas Cradle Song	97	2C
Christmastime	100	2C
Clouds	49	2B
Daddy's Lullaby	120	2C
Dance in a Circle	15	2A
Dance, Indian Man	140	2D
Dance, My Top!	150	2D
Dearest Child	122	2C
Debka Hora	145	2D
Drum Major, The	166	2D
Elves' Christmas Eve, The	98	2C
Escalator, The	24	2A
Go to Sleep	36	2A
Hanukkah Time	93	2B
Happy Birthday to You	85	2B
Happy River, The	21	2A
Have You Heard the Wind?	48	2B
Hen Who Quacked, The	134	2D
Here We Go Skating	29	2A
Hideaway Bunny	132	2D
House of the Mouse, The	136	2D
How Do You Do Today?	148	2D
Hunter, The	40	2A
Hurray for Halloween!	86	2B
I Know Amelia	139	2D
I Like to Make Up Songs (Unit)	110	
I Like to Sing	7	2A
If You Can't Say Something Nice	70	2B
I'll Call Him Bambi	69	2B
Indian Lullaby	125	2C
It's Music Time Again	137	2D
It's So Nice on the Ice	78	2B
Jingle at the Windows	154	2D
Jolly Party, A	106	2C
Kind Mister Cobbler	33	2A
Leaf Kites	47	2A
Lights	52	2B
Little April Shower	75	2B
Little Bird on My Window	126	2C
Little Chick	131	2D
Little Man in the Wood	64	2B
Little Old Tugboat	161	2D
Little Sir Echo	50	2B
Little Wind	39	2A
Magic Bell Song	145	2D
Magic Mountain, The (Dance-A-Story)	167	
Magic of Musical Sound, The (Unit)	44	
March of the Little Flags	9	2A
Merry Christmas!	97	2C
Moonlight (key of C)	20	2A
Moonlight (key of F)	34	2A
Morning Bells	25	2A
Musette	144	2D
Music Time (Unit)	137	

SELECTION	PAGE	ALBUM	SELECTION	PAGE	ALBUM
My Donkey	130	2D	Sleep, Baby, Sleep!	121	2C
My Little Red Drum	10	2A	Slumber Bells	37	2A
My Mother	123	2C	Slumber Boat, The	124	2C
My Wish	127	2D	Snowflakes	54	2B
			Special Valentine, A	107	2C
Nightingale, The	62	2B	Spring Magic	58	2B
Norfolk Chimes	143	2D	Spring Song	66	2B
Now It Is Yule	96	2C	Stand Up!	84	2B
			Stars	53	2B
O Christmas Tree	94	2C	Star-Spangled Banner, The	116	2C
O Come, All Ye Faithful	102	2C			
O Come, Little Children	101	2C	Thank You	91	2B
O Little Town of Bethlehem	103	2C	Thanksgiving	89	2B
On the Bridge of Avignon	157	2D	Thanksgiving Day	90	2B
One, Two, Three	31	2A	Through the Forest	72	2B
Our Flag	119	2C	To Paree	158	2D
Out among the Fir Trees	28	2A	Tommy	129	2D
			Très Jolie Waltz	144	2D
Pick a Pumpkin	87	2B	Twinkle, Twinkle, Little Star	26	2A
Pumpkin Face	88	2B			
Puppet Show, The	138	2D	Wake-Up Clock, The	128	2D
			We Wish You a Merry Christmas	104	2C
Rain-Dance Song	163	2D	Westminster Chimes	143	2D
Riddle Song	141	2D	Wind, The	56	2B
Ring-ting-tingle	17	2A			
Rockabye Song, A	32	2A	Yankee Doodle	118	2C
See the Little Ducklings	22	2A			
Seesaw	159	2D			
Silent Night	103	2C			
Six Little Ducks	135	2D			
Skip to My Lou	152	2D			

"Dance-A-Story about The Magic Mountain," with music and narration, is available on RCA Victor long-play record LE-103 and may be purchased through Ginn and Company.

Index of First Lines of Poems

A candle looked up at the sky and said, (from "Candle Star") *Lourena Renton Brown*, 52

Every morning when the sun (from "This Happy Day") · *Harry Behn*, 90

I wake up in the morning early, (from "Singing Time") · *Rose Fyleman*, 128

If I (from "Wouldn't You?") · *John Ciardi*, 48

If you see a package (from "Secrets") · *E. Kathryn Fowler*, 100

Long ago—maybe a week or so— (from "Long Ago—Maybe a Week or So") · *Annette Wynne*, 59

On tip-toe comes the gentle dark (from "Good Night") · *Dorothy Mason Pierce*, 122

Owls and witches, (from "Halloween Magic") · *E. K. Merriam*, 86

There's magic in music, (from "There's Magic in Music") · *L. E. Watters*, 13

What sweeter music can we bring (from "Herrick's Carol") · *Robert Herrick*, 102

EFGH–076
PRINTED IN THE UNITED STATES OF AMERICA

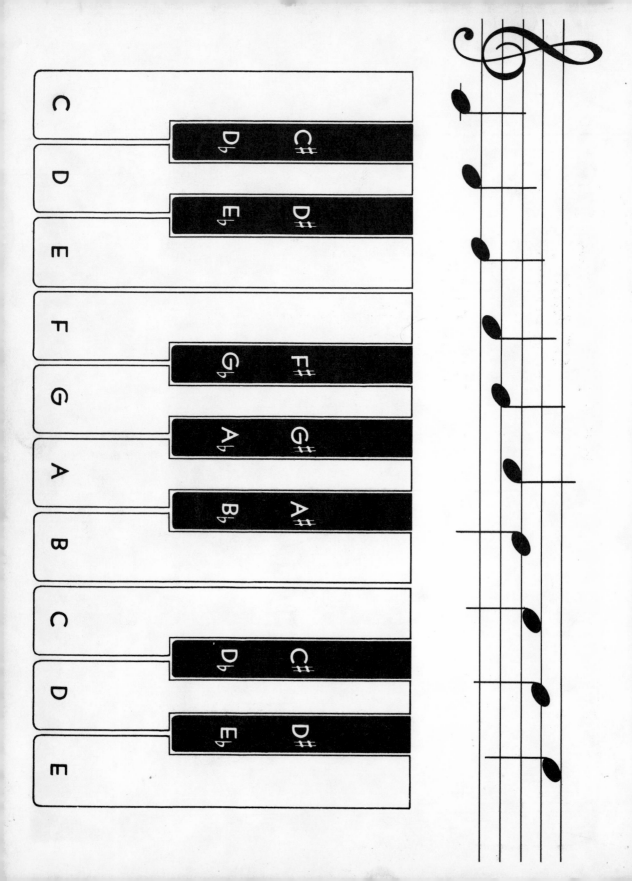